# The Homophobic Mind

by Wayne R. Dynes

New York

ISBN: 978-1-304-61542-8

# Contents

## II    *Biological Factors*     *74*

*Dedicated to the memory of my incomparable friend, Warren Johansson (1934-1994).*

# Introduction

The following pages address a host of myths and fabrications that have served over the centuries to rationalize prejudice and discrimination targeting GLBT people. This topic is disturbing and repellent, but it must be confronted head-on.

Viewed in context, the picture is not that bad – at least not as much as it was. Some years ago, when I first began to ponder these issues, a heartening conclusion had already surfaced. Much progress had been made in retiring the most absurd and unviable myths. Some seemed to have faded gradually and died (or so it seemed) of old age. Others, such as the idea that homosexuals suffer from impaired functioning, have retreated in the face of social-science findings that clearly indicate otherwise.

There are also some myths that are essentially innocuous, such as the notion that the word gay derives from "good as you" and swag comes from "secretly we are gay." The worst that can be said of them is that they are false etymologies.

Regrettably, the notions discussed below are not harmless.

With the current improvement in the intellectual climate, at least in advanced industrial countries, one might have expected that such archaic thought-patterns would all wither and disappear. Regrettably, that has not happened– at least not with any consistency across the board.

Not infrequently, the myths show a zombie-like tendency to revive, even when we had assumed, reasonably enough, that they had disappeared for good. A case in point concerns natural disasters, where various Christian ministers - and some Jewish rabbis as well - blame hurricanes, earthquakes, droughts and other such upsets on our society's growing tolerance for homosexuality. They base their observations on current events. And yet they really don't, for in fact, this theme goes back almost 1500 years, to the Byzantine emperor Justinian.

So there is good reason to examine these hurtful motifs as carefully as we can, tracing their historical evolution and analyzing their flaws in evidence and reasoning.

The history of homophobia - to use the current, though somewhat problematic term - is not monolithic. Insidiously, the complex examined here comprises more than forty separate threads. The threads have very disparate origins, stemming from religion, philosophy, medicine, psychology, and folklore.

Yet they mostly flourish, if that is the appropriate term, in Western culture, starting in ancient Israel and ancient Greece and migrating to medieval and modern Europe, including its overseas offshoots.

Much of the rest of the world has happily escaped this blight. An anti-homosexual text from Zoroastrianism may be an exception. Moreover, anti-homosexual attitudes have been noted among the Manchus, as well as the Aztecs and the Incas. Yet these peoples, exceptional in this realm, do not seem to have been widely influential.

Recently, an argument has appeared that challenges this general principle of the Western locus of anti-homosexual attitudes. That is the claim of some contemporary Third World politicians and theorists that their lands were free of the taint of such vices until they were forced on them by corrupt colonizers from Europe. Even this notion is, however, of Western origin.

So we are left with the conclusion that this not-so-proud heritage is essentially a property of the West, and not the Rest. Why should this be so? I can only offer two tentative suggestions. The first points to monotheism. The three religions that have typically harbored aversion to same-sex love–Judaism, Christianity, and Islam–all share this belief in one God. Monotheism usually counts as an advance over the polytheistic belief systems it supplanted. Recent research, however, has shown that monotheism generally began with an attitude of fierce intolerance directed towards those who did no share the theology. Much emphasis was placed on the various commandments and behavioral rules enjoined

11

by the faith.

In their prime, monotheisms have not been noted for their capacity to embrace a policy of live and let live. Instead, they adhered to Augustine of Hippo's precept of "compelle intrare"–compel them [the heretics and the nonbelievers] to enter the fold. As outsiders, homosexuals were destined to fall afoul of these repressive measures. Outwardly at least, they had to conform to the prevailing norms, in sexual conduct as well as in belief.

In addition to monotheism, there is another conditioning factor - at first sight one that is less likely. That is democracy. A leading feature of the democratic ideal as it has matured is the imperative of equality, the idea that the claims of citizenship are universal, so that no special groups should remain apart. The corollary, at least according to one egalitarian version, is this. Since the majority are heterosexual, then everyone should be. This ideal of sociosexual uniformity fostered repression of same-sex behavior in Stalin's Soviet Union and Mao's China - even though those societies could nowadays scarcely be characterized as democratic.

What then of ancient Greece, where pederasty flourished? In fact the ancient Greeks were not egalitarian, since they tended to deny full rights to women, resident foreigners, and of course to slaves. With regard to homosexuality the Greeks were not always consistent. They tended to accept the behavior only in its intergenerational form (pederasty), commonly expressing disapproval of relations between two adult men. Moreover, in The Laws, Plato's second blueprint of the ideal society (after The Republic), the philosopher originated the notion that homosexual behavior was wrong because it was unnatural.

Thus the conditioning factors- the soil in which the evil flowers of homophobia grew - reflect ideals that are, broadly speaking, those of uniformity. Monotheists demand allegiance to one God, and all the ordinances that that monarch of the universe is presumed to have enacted. All too often, egalitarians expect everyone to be the same, in rights, in income, and in sexuality.

How can we best approach the complex story of the repression of a major sexual minority? Meme theory may help. A meme may be characterized as "an idea, behavior or style that spreads from person to person within a culture." A meme serves as a vehicle for conveying cultural ideas, symbols or practices, which can be transmitted from one mind to another through writing, speech, gestures, rituals or other imitable phenomena. Advocates of the concept regard memes as cultural analogues to genes in that they self-replicate, mutate, and respond to selective pressures.

A common misperception is that there is a biological mechanism for the transmission of memes. Yet there is not: they are a purely cultural phenomenon. The term was coined by the British evolutionary biologist Richard Dawkins in *The Selfish Gene* (1976) as a tool for exploring evolutionary principles in tracing the spread of ideas and cultural phenomena. Examples of memes given in Dawkins' book included melodies, catch-phrases, fashion, and the technology of building arches.

Since Dawkins' time, the meme approach has been found useful in all sorts of studies, from racial prejudice and religious beliefs to urban legends and "viral" motifs on the Internet.

The overall approach is termed mimetics. Memes are not static, but operate through the processes of variation, mutation, competition, and inheritance, all of them influencing a meme's reproductive success. Memes spread through the behaviors that they generate in their hosts. Memes that propagate less prolifically may become extinct, while others may survive, spread, and (for better or for worse) mutate. In this view memes that replicate most effectively enjoy more success, and some may replicate effectively even when they prove to be detrimental to the welfare of their hosts. Some commentators have likened memes to contagion, as exemplified by fads, hysteria, copycat crimes, and copycat suicides.

Still in the course of development, meme theory has encountered some criticisms. At this point it may best be regarded as a hermeneutic tool rather than a fully formed scientific theory. At all events, in this study the concept is useful in serving to characterize the great variety of anti-homosexual beliefs and attitudes, disentangling them from the monocausal illusion that there is one single, unified phenomenon termed "homophobia."

Just as these homonegative memes are diverse, so too are those who subscribe to them. The most important contingent is made up of the "traditional-values" people. Most of them are religious, consisting chiefly of evangelical Christians, the hierarchy of the Catholic church, Orthodox Jews,

14

and some Muslims. Others in this composite group, while detached from religion, may nonetheless maintain that the social fabric demands that traditional values be upheld.

Psychiatrists were once a major factor. Yet since the 1973 decision by the American Psychiatric Association to remove homosexuality from the list of disorders, this negativity has much diminished among them. In the past, though, psychiatrists were major contributors to the medicalization of same-sex behavior, originating a number of the memes. These fabrications still circulate, even after their abandonment by the groups that originated them.

Totalitarians, both fascists and Communists, readily embraced the motif of decadence–homosexuality as a mark of social disintegration. Fortunately, these political extremists have lost much of their power. Nonetheless, the skinheads in Western Europe, and neofascist parties in general, represent a worrisome set of survivals.

Finally, the ranks of the perpetrators include, regrettably, some gay people themselves. Some poor souls are browbeaten into internalizing the homophobic motifs. Common in other minority groups as well, this practice is sometimes termed self-inferiorization. Some gay and lesbian people cherish notions that enhance a sense of victimhood, such as the misconception that the word faggot derives from medieval burnings of sodomites. We have made great progress in combating the slur that same-sex behavior is "abnormal." Oddly enough, some queer theorists do not find this erasure to their liking. Decrying "homonormativity," they assert that the desire to assimilate has the effect of stigmatizing those whose sexualities do not conform to standards of normalcy.

In scrutinizing the anti-homosexual motifs that are here under the microscope, the older ideas of stereotypes and of prejudice are sometimes useful. Yet these terms fail to capture the protean malleability of the homonegative motifs, which have proven all-too-resilient in their capacity to adapt to changing cultural settings as they undergo variation, mutation, and reshaping in competition with related ideas.

Most of the memes discussed in this text concern gay men. Historically, these notions were, by and large, not thought to apply to lesbians. There are some lesbian-only stereotypes, e.g. the notion that there are no true lesbians, because those who adopt this lifestyle are simply women who are too homely or socially awkward to attract a man. Sometimes "good Samaritan" jocks will seek to "prove" this assertion by seducing lesbians. Ignoring protests, the would-be seducers claim that their victims welcome their gross attentions. In the last analysis, however, dislike of lesbians needs to be studied in the context of attitudes that demean all women - regrettably, a very large subject. That task will not be attempted in these pages.

For some the term "homosexual" now seems old-fashioned. Yet it is not inappropriate for the material, which reached critical mass in an era different from out own. One must keep this difference in mind, all the while acknowledging the hardiness of the motifs that have survived into the present era.

In the sections that follow sometimes I use the word gay in addition to homosexual; at other times, when a more inclusive perspective is required, GLBT (gay, lesbian, bisexual, and trans).

There remains this nagging question, At this late date, why bring out this dusty old bric-à-brac? Surely, in the early twenty-first century our enhanced understanding has thoroughly demolished this outdated rubbish and everything that pertains to it. The answer is that we have advanced, but as yet not far enough.

An ambiguous role has been played by Queer Theory, a plant that thrives in academia. Hobbled by its addiction to jargon and paradox, Queer Theory has not been successful in breaking out of recondite circles. The general public is unaware of it, and will probably remain so.

Three books that address the problem of homonegativity deserve mention. The first is *Homophobia: A History* by Byrne R. S. Fone (New York, 2000). Despite the title, this work turns out to be a narrative of the mainstream of gay history in the Western tradition from ancient times to the present. Instances of homophobia occur only in passing, representing no more than a series of many speed-bumps along the way. While this book serves to place the motifs in time, it does little to clarify their inner motivation.

Another work is the *Dictionnaire de l'homophobie,* edited by Louis-Georges Tin (Paris, 2003; there is also an English-language version). This alphabetically arranged volume provides some useful articles on individual countries and regions. However, the coverage of the motifs (memes) is patchy and incomplete.

In Feb., 2013, the American philosopher John Corvino brought out a new book, *What's Wrong with Homosexuality?* (Oxford University Press), tackling some of the major anti-homosexual arguments. Written in an easy conversational style and wearing its learning lightly, this book addresses some of the problems ordinary people have raised with him over a period of twenty years in which Professor Corvino has been lecturing and debating. The volume is brief, 153 pages, and the author takes up a good deal of his space recounting personal anecdotes, some quite relevant, others less so. Ultimately, the focus is narrow, being concerned primarily with the morality of homosexuality. As will be clear from the following discussion, many of the anti-homosexual memes are not directed primarily at issues of morality. They are a much more diverse lot, encompassing religious, sociological, psychological, and biological themes, among others. Still, John Corvino's book serves as a useful introduction to the issues.

# *Two problematic terms: Homophobia and Heterosexism*

With the rise of the gay political movement in the late 1960s, the condemnation of homosexuality as immoral, criminal, and sick came under increasing scrutiny. When the American Psychiatric Association abandoned homosexuality as a psychiatric diagnosis in 1973, the question of why some heterosexuals harbor strongly negative attitudes toward homosexuals began to receive serious scholarly consideration.

The immediate precursor of the term "homophobia" was "homoerotophobia," introduced by Wainwright Churchill in his 1967 book *Homosexual Behavior Among Males* in 1967. Several years later two psychologists realized that the expression would be more effective if it were shortened. The first known usage of "homophobia" was by Kenneth Smith in an article in *Psychological Reports* (no.29) for 1971. George Weinberg, who claims to have coined the word before Smith's usage, has tirelessly promoted it, as in his 1972 book *Society and the Healthy Homosexual*. Weinberg used the term homophobia to characterize heterosexuals' dread of being in close quarters with homosexuals as well as homosexuals' self loathing.

The *American Heritage Dictionary* (1992 edition) defines homophobia as "aversion to gay or homosexual people or their lifestyle or culture" and "behavior or an act based on this aversion." Other definitions identify homophobia as an irrational fear of same-sex behavior.

The introduction of the term served to turn the tables on critics of homosexuality, who routinely castigated it as a mental illness. As homophobes, though, they might be the ones suffering from a mental disorder. By drawing popular and scientific attention to the virulence of irrational anti-gay hostility, the creation of this term marked a watershed. Nevertheless, it bears significant limitations.

19

As Gregory M. Herek, professor of psychology at the University of California, Davis, has observed, the term homophobia is problematic for several reasons.

First, empirical research has not demonstrated that heterosexuals' antigay attitudes may reasonably be considered a phobia in the clinical sense. In fact, the available data suggest that many heterosexuals who express hostility toward gay men and lesbians do not manifest the physiological reactions to homosexuality that are associated with other phobias.

Secondly, the use of the term homophobia implies that antigay prejudice is an individual, clinical entity more than it is a social phenomenon fostered by long-standing ideologies and patterns of intergroup relations.

Finally, a phobia is usually experienced as dysfunctional and unpleasant. Yet antigay prejudice has, sad to say, commonly been highly functional for the heterosexuals who manifest it. Through their open hostility they consolidate their relations with others of like mind.

A related term is "heterosexism," first introduced in 1971. Heterosexism characterizes an amalgam of attitudes, bias, and discrimination that privilege opposite-sex sexuality and relationships. The term can include the presumption that everyone is heterosexual or, less drastically, the idea that opposite-sex attractions and relationships are the only norm and therefore superior. Although heterosexism is defined in the online editions of the *American Heritage Dictionary of the English Language* and the *Merriam-Webster*

*Collegiate Dictionary* as anti-gay discrimination and/or prejudice "by heterosexual people" and "by heterosexuals," people of any sexual orientation can hold such attitudes and
bias. The first published use of the term was in 1971 by
the New York-based bookseller and gay-rights activist Craig
Rodwell.

The use of the term heterosexism suggests parallels between antigay sentiment and other forms of prejudice, such
as racism, antisemitism, and sexism. In particular, it has
been argued that the concept of heterosexism is similar to
the concept of racism in that both ideas exalt privilege for
society's dominant groups. For example, borrowing from
the racial concept of white privilege, the concept of heterosexual privilege has been applied to single out benefits of
(presumed) heterosexuality within society that heterosexuals take for granted. Yet the parallels between heterosexism,
on the one hand, and racism, antisemitism, and sexism, on
the other, must not be overstressed, for each of these forms
of prejudice has its own history and distinctive valences.

Variants are "heterocentrism" and "heterosexualism."

Although the term heterosexism is often explained as a
coinage modeled on sexism, the derivation points more to
(1) heterosex(ual) + -ism than (2) hetero- + sexism. In
fact, the portmanteau word heterosexualism often serves as
an equivalent to sexism and racism.

Given this lack of semantic transparency, researchers,
outreach workers, critical theorists and GLBT activists have
adopted a whole array of terms, such as institutionalized ho-

mophobia, state(-sponsored) homophobia, sexual prejudice, anti-gay bigotry, straight privilege, compulsory heterosexuality. Note also homonormativity and (from gender theory and queer theory) heteronormativity.

This profusion of terms suggests a certain conceptual volatility, reflecting the fact that the vocables are often wielded more as rhetorical devices than a genuine tools of analysis.

Although usage of the words has not been uniform, homophobia has typically been employed to describe individual antigay attitudes and behaviors; while heterosexism points to societal-level ideologies and patterns of institutionalized oppression of non-heterosexual people.

Reflecting on the problems posed by this word cloud, Gregory M. Herek has proposed the term "sexual prejudice." As he remarks, "Broadly conceived, sexual prejudice refers to all negative attitudes based on sexual orientation, whether the target is homosexual, bisexual, or heterosexual. Given the current social organization of sexuality, however, such prejudice is almost always directed at people who engage in homosexual behavior or label themselves gay, lesbian, or bisexual . . . Conceptualizing heterosexuals' negative attitudes toward homosexuality and bisexuality as sexual prejudice – rather than homophobia – has several advantages [Herek continues]. First, sexual prejudice is a descriptive term. Unlike homophobia, it conveys no a priori assumptions about the origins, dynamics, and underlying motivations of antigay attitudes.

"Second, the term explicitly links the study of antigay hostility with the rich tradition of social psychological research on prejudice.

"Third, using the construct of sexual prejudice does not require value judgments that antigay attitudes are inherently irrational or evil." (G. M. Herek,"The Psychology of Sexual Prejudice," *Current Directions in Psychological Science*, 2000, no. 9, pp. 19-22).

This proposal deserves serious consideration. Yet such is the rhetorical punch of "homophobia" and "heterosexism,"that Herek's substitute, despite its merits, seems unlikely to supplant them. In this work we will tend to prefer "homonegativity," though sometimes another term will be appropriate.

*Note.* I first began to address these problems some twenty-five years ago, in concert with my learned friend, Warren Johansson, to whom this publication is dedicated. We worked so closely together that our ideas often merged. I have utilized some of these jointly-produced ideas here. Some passages in the following texts derive from earlier publications that are copyright by me, especially the *Encyclopedia of Homosexuality*, New York: Garland, 1990. There is also some factual material stemming from non-copyright sources available on the Internet.

With a few exceptions, Internet links are not provided here because over time the sites are subject to modification or disappearance.

# Part I
# Religious and Philosophical Aspects

## 1  *Homosexuality is unnatural.*

*The Charge.*  Being heterosexual means doing what comes naturally.  As Chicago's Cardinal Francis George opined early in 2013 that is the "way that nature operates."  In a Christmas message a few weeks before, Pope Benedict XVI decried gay marriage, saying that it destroyed the "essence of the human creature."  He stressed that a person's gender identity is God-given and unchangeable.  Those seeking to institute gay marriage are engaging in a "manipulation of human nature."

"People dispute the idea that they have a nature, given to them by their bodily identity, that serves as a defining element of the human being," the pontiff declared.  "They deny their nature and decide that it is not something previously given to them, but that they make it for themselves." The pope singled out a precept of feminist author and philosopher Simone de Beauvoir –" "one is not born a woman, one becomes so" – " stigmatizing it as "the foundation for what is put forward today under the term 'gender' as a new philosophy of sexuality. According to this philosophy, sex is no longer a given element of nature, that man has to accept and personally make sense of: it is a social role

24

that we choose for ourselves, while in the past it was chosen for us by society. The profound falsehood of this theory and of the anthropological revolution contained within it is obvious."

Through long-standing practice the law has added its authoritative voice to this discussion. The "crime against nature" is an expression documented in published cases in the United States since 1814. Historically, the scope of this designation is broad, embracing a series of behaviors, including same-sex acts, anal sex, bestiality, incest, miscegenation, and necrophilia.

The expression "crime against nature" has also served as a synonym for sodomy or buggery. These last acts are prime instances of departure from Nature's wise ordinances.

***Historical Background.*** As Raymond Williams observed in *Keywords* (New York, 1976), the term "nature" is one of the most complex in the language; it is also one of the most dangerous.

Here we must attend also to the force of the emotionally charged antonym: the "unnatural," which needs to be distinguished from the supernatural and the praetematural, from second nature, and from the peculiarly Thomistic concept of the "connatural" (which, as the personal and habitual, stands in a kind of intermediate zone between the natural and the unnatural).

The ancient Greek word for nature, physis, was unique to that language and to Hellenic thought; no equivalent can be found in the Semitic and Oriental languages, or in other intellectual traditions. The term physis derives from a verb meaning "to grow," and hence retains strong connotations of organic completeness and development toward a goal. The primary notion of physis is a magical, autonomous life force manifesting itself not only in the creation and preservation of the universe, but even in the properties and character traits of species and individuals. Thus in medical usage it even leads into the sphere of the pharmacopoeia and of constitutional biology.

Its use among the Greeks can be best understood in the light of three contrasting pairs of terms: physis/nomos (law or custom); physis/techne (art); kata physin/para physin (against nature). The last of these antinomies, which is of particular significance for our enquiry, received a decisively influential formulation from the aged Plato (ca. 427-347 BCE) in his Laws. In this book the philosopher condemns same-sex relations because, unlike those in which animals naturally engage, they cannot lead to procreation ("[W[hen the male sex unites with the female for the purpose of procreation the pleasure so experienced is held to be according to nature, but when males unite with males or females with females, to be contrary to nature." The Laws I 636B-C; cf. also 836 B-839 A).

During the Hellenistic period this Greek idea found its way into the Testaments of the Twelve Patriarchs (a set of documents of evolving Judaism) and into the apologetic writings of Philo Judaeus, who equated the Mosaic Law with the "law of nature." These texts served to transmit the idea into the New Testament with the fateful formulation of Romans 1:26-27, which speaks of changing "the natural use to that which is unnatural." In due course, this language - which in the Pauline text cited sets the stage for a condemnation of male homosexuality - made its way into other contexts, including that of jurisprudence.

The path for this development was smoothed by the earlier Roman acceptance of the concept of "natural law," defined by Cicero as "right reason in agreement with nature." Cicero ascribed this law to God, hence giving legal standing to Biblical injunctions in the eyes of Christian interpreters, and went on to insist that "it is a sin to try to alter this law." On the other hand, the Christians tended to overlook Cicero's statement that in practice God is also the enforcing judge of natural law; that role they took on themselves. The twelfth-century groundswell of interpretation of Roman law and canon law had a major emphasis on natural law perspectives, both classical and Christian. Natural law underpinned arguments justifying anti-homosexual legislation throughout the Middle Ages and into early modern times, when its legacy passed from church to secular penology, retaining much of its influence. This secularization notwithstanding, natural-law arguments play a major role today in the continuing Roman Catholic condemnation of homosexual behavior.

It is curious that the notion of "crime against nature," familiar to us from the penal codes of the American states, did not figure in Henry VIII's English statute of 1533 or its successors. Yet Sir Edward Coke did include the expression

27

in his seventeenth-century Institutes and Reports, whence it passed into the Anglo-American legal tradition.

In medieval Europe the semantically iridescent concept of natura was perpetuated and even given some new variations and imagery by moralists (Peter Damian), literary figures (Bernard Silvestre, Alan of Lille, and Jean de Meun), and philosophers (Albertus Magnus and Thomas Aquinas). Later French usage coined the adjective antiphysique (taken into English in the rare "antiphysical") for unnatural sexual behavior.

Eighteenth-century aesthetics saw a broad shift from a view of nature as rule-obeying and rule-enforcing to one in which the awesome complexity and sovereign fecundity of nature was emphasized. This new orientation fostered the admiration which naturalists of today profess for the unspoiled wilderness, untrodden by man and unaltered by human hands. This shift is part of the change from neo-Classicism to Romanticism. By providing a more flexible definition of nature the new approach gave the idea new life as a normative (though more diffuse) principle.

The nineteenth and twentieth century witnessed a curious paradox. Conservative thinkers were generally unwavering in denouncing homosexuality as "unnatural" (Ezra Pound), while for their part some homophile apologists revived the ancient Hippocratic definition to claim that homosexuality is inborn and thus "natural" (K. H. Ulrichs, Magnus Hirschfeld). Today progressive thought favors natural foods and the environmental protection of nature, causes that would seem clearly to be valuable. But a latent conflict persists, for the sexual freedom and tolerance that the progressive sector cherishes have been historically denounced as "unnatural."

Recent years have seen the rise of the New Natural Law theorists in the academic world. The best known figures in this trend are Robert P. George of Princeton and John Finnis of Oxford. While these writers tend to accept the precepts of revealed religion (Christianity), they believe that many of the same results - though probably not all of them - can be achieved by the pure processes of reasoning. They thus leave some wiggle room for a more nuanced approach to same-sex orientation, though it is clear that they are not friendly to it.

*Response*. If nature is truly all-embracing, it is impossible to depart from it. Only things that do not exist at all, such as centaurs and phlogiston, would be unnatural. In this perspective, the supposed criterion of naturalness provides no means for separating existing acts that are judged licit from those regarded as illicit; some yardstick other than "naturalness" - since all acts possess that attribute - must be supplied.

Another approach classifies some things within the world as natural, while other are not. In practice, though, this binarism runs the risk of being culture-bound and subjective. Thus clothing, cosmetics, and airplanes have been sometimes stigmatized as unnatural. Perhaps they are. But then it is hard to see how, say, life-saving heart surgery can be regarded as anything other than an unnatural intervention in an otherwise inevitable process. How many proponents of "naturalness" would be willing to revert to a Stone Age economy and Stone Age medicine?

In order to buttress their position, opponents of so-called "unnatural" sex need to demonstrate that they have at their disposal a comprehensive and even-handed theory of the natural and its opposite. What usually happens in practice is that some other assumption, or assumptions, are imported to provide a basis of decision. Thus the natural-unnatural contrast becomes essentially a rhetorical device that supplies a pseudo-confirmation of moral presuppositions reached on quite other grounds.

Another critique reflects the fact that the image of Natura is a survival of the mother goddess figures of pagan antiquity, in which God is the male principle of creation and "Nature" the female counterpart. Discarding such relics of polytheism, modern scientific thought does not concern itself with the supposed "purposes" or "aims" of nature, and in general rejects teleological concepts as empirically undemonstrable. The standard claim is that nature has intended sexuality solely for the purpose of procreation and that any sexual pleasure obtained from non-procreative activity is therefore "unnatural" and wrongful. To this assertion it can be rejoined that only a tiny fraction of all human sexual activity has reproductive consequences, and that to restrict it to such a narrow goal would doom most of the population to virtually lifelong abstinence - though the ascetic ideal would regard such a state of affairs as a desirable end.

From a scientific perspective, the debate over the

30

"naturalness" of homosexuality was joined by the eminent sex researcher Alfred C. Kinsey. Maintaining that norms of naturalness are in the last analysis historically contingent and arbitrary, Kinsey concluded that anything sexual that can be done is natural. The older arguments deployed by theologians and moralists were, in his view, accompanied by a considerable charge of emotionality. "This has been effected, in part, by synonymizing the terms clean, natural, normal, moral, and right, and the terms unclean, unnatural, abnormal, immoral, and wrong."

A key feature of traditional efforts to affirm the nature standard in human sexuality has been gender dimorphism: the idea that male and female are completely distinct, each in its own way devoted to the pursuit of the opposite sex. Ostensibly, this binarism is an absolute norm. Thus has it always been and thus it always will be. Yet more recent biological studies have indicated that there are intermediate types. In this light some researchers have concluded there are more than two genders - as many as five. Others, who would not go that far, acknowledge that the traditional categories are too rigid, and provide an incomplete picture of the full range of human variation. Even focusing on the male and female poles of the spectrum, we find considerable variations within each category. This new concept of fluidity of gender leads inexorably to a recognition of the complexities of sexual orientation. That too may be fluid. It seems increasingly clear then that there are no fixed roles assigned to the genders.

Other perspectives have been disclosed by Queer Theory, though these remain controversial. The term "gender performativity" was advanced by the post-structuralist theorist Judith Butler in her 1990 book *Gender Trouble*. She characterizes gender as the effect of reiterated acting, a pattern that produces the impression of a stable or normal gender while obscuring the contradiction and instability of any single person's gender posture. According to Butler, this gambit flourishes within a much larger sphere of performativity. Earlier exponents of a similar approach had written of the dramaturgic model of social relations. In this view we are always enacting roles rather than following any fixed imperatives of behavior.

Anthropologists have reported homosexuality in many tribal societies (presumably "close to nature"); a wide range of ethologists have described homosexuality among other species (presumed more "natural"); and theorists in sociobiology have sought to provide an evolutionary rationale for human homosexuality. Perhaps as a reflection of these efforts as well as of other scientific embarrassments involving earlier cultural assumptions about "naturalness," it is no longer scientifically respectable to maintain the argument against homosexuality as "unnatural." This development has not yet had a major impact on Judeo-Christian homophobia, popular demagogic rhetoric, and public opinion among the less educated. Over time, though, this improved understanding may be expected to undermine the credibility of the position that "homosexuality is unnatural."

As regards the law, the 2003 US Supreme Court decision in the Lawrence case invalidated the remaining provisions in the law of some states sanctioning the so-called "crime against nature."

**BIBLIOGRAPHY**. A. P. d'Entrèves, Natural Law, London: Longmans, 1951; Alfred C. Kinsey, et al., "Concepts of Normality and Abnormality in Sexual Behavior," in P. H. Hoch and J. Zubin, eds., Psychological Development in Health and Disease, New York: Grune and Stratton, 1949, pp. 11-32; C. S. Lewis, Studies in Words, Cambridge: Cambridge University Press, 1960, pp. 24-74; Arthur O. Lovejoy, " 'Nature' as Aesthetic Norm," in his Essays in the History of Ideas, Baltimore: Johns Hopkins University Press, 1948, pp. 69-77; Clément Rosset, L'Anti-nature, Paris: Presses Universitaires de France, 1973: Pim Pronk, Against Nature: Types of Moral Argumentation Regarding Homosexuality, Grand Rapids, MI: Eerdmans, 1993.

## 2  *Only sexual acts that can lead to procreation are acceptable; homosexual conduct - like bestiality and anal and oral heterosexual coitus - does not fulfill this condition.*

*The Charge.*  The procreation standard was perceptively formulated by Plato in The Laws:"[T]his law of ours . . . permits sexual intercourse solely according to nature for the purpose of having children and forbids it with the male, wherein the human race is intentionally murdered, together with the sowing of seed on rocks and stones where it can never take root and produce new individuals."  The Laws, VIII 836 B-839 A; cf. 636 B-C).

As Alfred North Whitehead remarked, all of Western philosophy consists of footnotes to Plato. That is certainly true in this instance.

*Historical Background.*  It is commonly thought that a dour, restrictive view of sexual ethics is enshrined in the Hebrew Bible and the New Testament.  Yet it is hard to find a clear statement to that effect in any of those ancient religious documents.  In fact there is plenty of contrary evidence.  Proverbs 5:15-19 encourages couples to enjoy sexual pleasure together within marriage.  Even though he was conflicted about sexuality, the apostle Paul nonetheless says

34

that husbands and wives should render the sexual affection due each other - "refraining only during times set aside for prayer and fasting" (1 Corinthians 7:3-5).

In fact the long-dominant religious arguments in favor of limiting sexual acts to those that can lead to procreation were created by Early Christian writers of the Patristic period, though they drew on their interpretations of the Septuagint and Philo of Alexandria. This amalgam of sex-negative views generally sheltered under the umbrella concept of "porneia" or fornication, which had highly negative connotations. Sexual promiscuity was stigmatized by linking it with heathen rites, termed "spiritual adultery." Philo, Tatian, and Clement reinterpreted Paul's conflicted thoughts, giving them a restrictive emphasis and blending them with Platonic analyses of desire. Yet Clement's contemporary Epiphanes focused more on Platonic and Stoic communal sexual ideals.

Thomas Aquinas (*Summa Theologiae*, II-II, q. 154, 11) rejects bestiality, homosexuality, and "unnatural" heterosexual intercourse as departures from the proper species, the proper gender, and the proper organ(s) respectively. How was this concept of propriety–or finality as it is called in some recent Vatican documents–determined? Such a neat scheme does not derive from the Bible, which in its formative stage (the Hebrew Bible) is innocent of the concept of nature and the unnatural. It must depend on an overarching concept of teleology, that is say, the assumptions that the universe works towards some great and final purpose; that this purpose has been worked out in every detail; and that moreover it is perfectly accessible to human reason. Yet modern science rejects such a teleological worldview.

Hovering in the background of the procreation standard appears also to be a simplistic folk notion that each organ must have a single basic function to which others may be added only at one's peril. Yet the genitals already serve two purposes - elimination and copulation - why not then the anus? As the Marquis de Sade pointed out long ago, if Nature truly wished to forbid anal intercourse, she would have placed the orifice in a position that would make it inaccessible to the erect penis.

Defenders of the procreation-only thesis must also cope with the habits of kissing, caressing, and other types of foreplay which, although they have traditionally been accepted as licit, in no way permit procreation in and of themselves. (It is revealing of the debt of Freudian psychoanalysis to religious tradition that it has sought to consider "unnatural" acts acceptable only if they lead to and enhance coitus, with its procreation potential.) There is also, of course, the matter of contraception and birth control. In fact the play element in culture has always held an important place in heterosexual behavior even as narrowly defined by Aquinas; to attempt some tortueous scheme for excluding it under some conditions and permitting it in others is special pleading.

In recent discussions concerning same-sex marriage opponents have advanced a version of the procreation argument. According to law professor Dale Carpenter (who is critical of this view), it can be stated this way: "Procreation is indispensable to human survival. Marriage is for procreation, and procreation should occur within marriage. Procreation is the one important attribute of marriage that supplies the male-female definition. Gay couples can't procreate as a couple, so gay couples shouldn't be allowed to marry."

Gay-marriage advocates respond as follows. Since procreation has never been required for marriage, the premise that "marriage is for procreation" is wrong, or at least incomplete. Sterile couples, old couples, and couples who simply don't want to procreate are all allowed to marry. No-one objects to their marriages, so no-one should on this ground object to same-sex marriages. Opponents of gay marriage have attempted to respond to this point, but their arguments have not carried conviction.

*Response*. Narrow procreation-only standards do not hold up for one simple reason. Society has always permitted sexual relations between two persons who cannot have children, whether because of impotence, injury, or advanced age.

**BIBLIOGRAPHY**. John T. Noonan, Jr., Contraception: A History of Its Treatment by the Catholic Theologians and Canonists, Cambridge: Harvard University Press, 1965; Michel Foucault, The Use of Pleasure (The History of Sexuality, Vol. 2), New York: Pantheon, 1985; Kathy L. Gaca, The Making of Fornication: Eros, Ethics, and Political Reform in Greek Philosophy and Early Christianity, Berkeley: University of California Press, 2003.

# 3   *God made Adam and Eve, not Adam and Steve.*

*The Charge.* The conservative Christian slogan "God made Adam and Eve, not Adam and Steve" may seem trivial, but actually it makes an important point, for it epitomizes Bible-based arguments that tell conclusively against homosexual behavior. Among other things, the statement affirms that the Biblical account of the creation of human beings as a male-female pair, as narrated in the book of Genesis, indicates the natural way of life for humanity.

*Background.* The phrase about Adam and Steve appeared on a 1977 protest sign, as noted in a New York Times report concerning a November 19 rally in Houston that year. Two years later Jerry Falwell included it in a press conference. A report in *Christianity Today* gave the utterance wide circulation.

The phrase continued to reverberate. In it is now widely familiar and, when used to name two characters in a work of fiction, signals that they are members of a homosexual pair (cf. Paul Rudnick's play "The Most Fabulous Story Ever Told," the 2005 film "Adam & Steve," and other works).

The key passage in the Bible is Genesis 2:18-22 where we are told that God decided that Adam needed a "helper." Some translations use the terms "companion," "helpmate," or "partner" here. God marched all of the animals past Adam, looking for a suitable helper, but none was found.

So God put Adam to sleep, removed one of his ribs and created Eve from the bone.

Although this implies a cloning operation, it obviously was not, because Adam, being a male, had XY sex chromosomes; Eve was a female with XX chromosomes. This example shows the need to place the biblical narrative within the realm of biological reality, correcting it where necessary.

For their part, conservative Christians insist on their own interpretation: God created Eve to be Adam's wife. He made a woman to be the companion of Adam, a male. This indicates God's plan for humanity, which is simply that men and women are to pair off, and form permanent, heterosexual partnerships.

*Response*. Keeping within the Biblical framework, if either Adam or Eve were homosexual - that is, a Kinsey 6, exclusively so - the human race would not have developed. God obviously needed to create both Adam and Eve as individuals with a heterosexual capacity, so that they could be fruitful and multiply, and fill the earth with human progeny, even though that required their children to commit incest. But did he need to make them exclusively heterosexual?

In verse 18, God observes: "It is not good for the man to be alone" (NIV). This shows the importance that God ascribed to committed relationships. For a heterosexual person, the suitable companion is an individual of the opposite gender. For a homosexual person, the suitable companion is a person of the same gender. To say that gays and lesbians should not form committed relationships is to imply that it is good for people to remain alone. This would seem to be a direct contradiction of God's precept.

As far as continuation of the species goes, Adam and Steve can indeed have progeny, either through adoption or with the assistance of a surrogate mother. Lesbians, of course, can become mothers themselves, and many do.

**BIBLIOGRAPHY.** Matt Ridley, The Red Queen: Sex and the Evolution of Human Nature, New York: Harper Perennial, 2003; Joseph Blenkinsopp, Creation, Un-creation, Recreation: A Discursive Commentary on Genesis 1-11, New York: Continuum, 2011.

# 4  *Homosexuality offends the cosmic order, causing earthquakes, plagues, and hurricanes.*

*The Charge*.  Homosexual conduct brings disaster on any society that is foolish enough to condone it.  This consequence is shown by the recent prevalence of hurricanes and floods in the United States, where the incidence of homosexuality has been increasing alarmingly.

On the June 8, 1998 edition of his television show, the evangelist Pat Robertson denounced Orlando, Florida, and Disney World for allowing "Gay Days." Robertson stated that the acceptance of homosexuality could result in hurricanes, earthquakes, tornadoes, terrorist bombings, and "possibly a meteor." Robertson returned to the theme on June 24, when he quoted the Book of Revelation to support his claims.

*Historical Background*.  A little known work of Hellenistic Judaism, *The Testament of Naftali* (ca. 100 BCE). combined several themes: idolatry and contumacy against the divine will; defiance of the cosmic order; and the sin of Sodom.  The putative destruction of that city by fire and brimstone in Lot's time provided the core for the gradual assemblage of a catalog of disasters ostensibly called down by same-sex behavior.

A further stage in the growth of these legends stems from the Christian emperor Justinian I, who ruled the Eastern

Roman Empire from 527 to 565. In 538 this homophobic ruler issued a law (Novella 77), which condemned sodomites to death "lest, as a result of these impious acts, whole cities should perish together with their inhabitants," a reference to the destruction of the Cities of the Plain, as recounted in the book of Genesis. The edict spoke of "diabolical and unlawful lusts," maintaining that because of such crimes there are famines, earthquakes, and pestilences. In Justinian's view same-sex acts are not simply immoral - they constitute a grave danger to the body politic.

By the seventeenth century learned prejudice and folk credulity had assembled a roster of no fewer than six such homo-catastrophes: earthquakes, famine, plague, Saracen incursions, large field-mice, and floods. (Noted by Benedict Carpzov, in his *Practicae novae imperialis Saxonicae rerum criminalium*, 1658.)

The televangelist Rev. Pat Robertson has remarked that the disaster of 9/11 came about as a result of America's tolerance of "abortionists, feminists, gays and lesbians." (He could have noted, following the old list, that "Saracen incursions" would surely occur.) His remarks were echoed by the Rev. Jerry Falwell, who has since been called to his maker.

Rev. John C. Hagee is a controversial Texas televangelist who regards the Catholic church as the "Great Whore of Babylon." He also claimed that God sent Hurricane Katrina to New Orleans to punish the city for hosting a thriving gay and lesbian culture.

What all the commentators leave out, however, is what

has been noted above: such arguments go all the way back to the emperor Justinian (527-565), who held that tolerance of same-sex behavior caused God to visit earthquakes on his realm. Stop the behavior, he believed, and the earthquakes would cease.

In a general sense these views reflect the Biblical pattern of the Prophet Jonah, who was thrown overboard to avoid shipwreck. More specific to homosexuality are the repeated denunciations in the Hebrew Bible of the male sacred prostitution of the kedeshim, an activity that was thought to incur Yahweh's displeasure. (I am aware that a recent revisionist school claims that the kedeshim did not engage in sex; I find this assertion unconvincing.)

In 2012 the following comment was making the rounds of the Internet net.

"Thirteen months before 9/11, on the day New York City passed homosexual domestic partnership regulations, I joined a group of Rabbis at a City Hall prayer service, pleading with God not to visit disaster on the city of N.Y. We have seen the underground earthquake, tsunami, Katrina, and now Haiti. All this is in sync with a two thousand year old teaching in the Talmud that the practice of homosexuality is a spiritual cause of earthquakes. Once a disaster is unleashed, innocents are also victims just like in Chernobyl. We plead with saner heads in Congress and the Pentagon to stop sodomization of our military and our society. Enough is enough." – Rabbi Yehuda Levin, spokesman for the Rabbinical Alliance of America.

Does the Talmud in fact offer any support for the notion that homosexual conduct is "a spiritual cause" of earthquakes? Apparently it does, according to the expert opinion of *Tzvee.blogspot.com*. As Tzvee indicates, the relevant passage stems from Yerushalmi Berakot (9:2). In fact, the text asserts that earthquakes are brought on by any one of a number of acts, including disputes; not taking heave offering and tithes from your produce; and also because God is unhappy that the Temple lies in ruins and Jews are flocking to theaters and circuses.

Gay sex may also occasion the tremors. In Tzvee's translation, Said R. Aha, "[The earth quakes] on account of the sin of homosexual acts. God said, 'You made your genitals throb in an unnatural act. By your life, I shall shake the earth on account of [the act of] this person.'"

The canon of the Jerusalem Talmud was closed about 600 CE, two or three generations after the promulgation of Justinian's etiological speculations incorporated into Novella 77. Evidently the notion was still fresh at the start of the seventh century.

Unless an earlier Jewish source can be found - and none is known that directly makes this case - the Sages were channeling their hated enemy, the anti-Semite Justinian I. This would not be the first time that the rabbis borrowed from Christianity.

Finally, there is an Islamic parallel to these beliefs, though it is still imperfectly known. This incident comes from medieval Afghanistan. The poet Sanai of Ghazni (died ca. 1140) mocked the pederastic practices of his time, as embodied in the doings of the Khvaja of Herat. This man is depicted as profaning a holy place by taking his catamite there for a quick erotic encounter: "Not finding shelter, he became perturbed, The mosque, he reasoned, would be undisturbed." But he was discovered by a devout man, who, in his revulsion, echoed a traditional attack on same-sex relations:"These sinful ways of yours - that was his shout - have ruined all the crops and caused the drought!"

*Response*. All these claims rest on unproven links between individual conduct and the cosmic order. These claims are at variance with modern science. As such, they are the equivalent of urban legends.

# 5 *According to Leviticus, homosexuality is an abomination.*

*The Charge.* In Leviticus 18 and 20 the Bible defines homosexual conduct as abomination. Since Scripture is the Word of God, it must be so.

In this matter, the Reverend Fred Phelps, leader of the Westboro Baptist Church, minces no words, for he says simply: "God Hate Fags."

*Historical Background.* In contemporary usage the terms abomination and abominable refer in a generic way to something that is detestable or loathsome. Because of the Hebrew Bible usage, however - Leviticus 18:22, "Thou shalt not lie with mankind as with womankind: it is abomination" (cf. Leviticus 20:13; Deuteronomy 22:5 and 23:19; and I Kings 14:24) - the words retain a special association as part of the religious condemnation of male homosexual behavior. In Elizabethan English they were normally written "abhomination," "abhominable" as if they derived from Latin ab- and homo - hence "departing from the human; inhuman." In fact, the core of the Latin word is the religious term omen.

In any event the notion of abominatio(n) stems from its appearance in Jerome's Vulgate translation of the Bible, where it corresponds to Greek bdelygma and Hebrew to'ebah. The latter term denotes behavior that violates the covenant between God and Israel, and is applied to Canaanite trade practices, idolatry, and polytheism, among other offenses.

The aversion of the religious leaders of the Jewish community after the return from the Babylonian captivity to the "abominable customs" of their heathen neighbors, combined with the Zoroastrian prohibition of homosexual behavior, inspired the legal provisions added to the Holiness Code of Leviticus in the fifth century before the Christian era. In due course these became normative for Hellenistic Judaism and then for Pauline Christianity. The designation of homosexual relations as an "abomination" or "abominable crime" in medieval and modern sacral and legal texts echoes the wording of the Hebrew Bible.

The complex web of prohibitions recorded in the Book of Leviticus has defied full explanation from the standpoint of comparative religion. Recently influential among social scientists (though not among Biblical scholars) has been the interpretation of the anthropologist Mary Douglas *(Purity and Danger,* London, 1967), who views the category of abominations as part of a concern with the boundaries of classification. Strict adherence to these boundaries attests one's purity in relation to divinity.

***Response.*** Abomination is a religious category that has no proper place in determining the values of a secular society.

**BIBLIOGRAPHY**. James Milgrom, Leviticus 17-22, New Haven: Yale University Press, 2000.

47

# 6  *Homosexual conduct is inherently sinful.*

*The Charge.*    Many Christian denominations and a number of Evangelical ministers (such as Pat Robertson and Jerry Falwell) have aptly cited Biblical texts demonstrating that same-sex behavior is sinful.

These religious authorities hold that such carnal acts as anal and oral sex (along with fornication of any kind) are forms of sexual immorality that must be severely discouraged.  Still, this precept does not signal any disrespect to human persons, for we should should "love the sinner and not the sin."

That said, we must all be ever mindful of sin; its snares lurk everywhere.  If we fall into sinful homosexual behavior, we must repent and try our level best not to repeat it.

*Historical Background.*    In Abrahamic contexts - those of Judaism, Christianity and Islam - sin is the act of violating God's will. More generally, sin can also be viewed as anything within individuals that violates the ideal relationship between them and God.

Some crimes rank as sins, and some sins stand out as greater than others. In this nuanced concept, sins fall in a spectrum from minor errors to deadly misdeeds.  Catholicism regards the least corrupt sins as venial sins –" which are part of the hazards of human life, and carry little divine consequence, especially if the sinner sincerely repents. Conversely, sins of great evil are mortal mortal sins –" which bring the dire consequence of going to Hell if unrepented for. The branch of theology that studies sin is called hamartiology.

The unforgivable sin (or eternal sin) is a grave infraction that can never be expunged, Some moralists believe that same-sex behavior falls in this category.

For centuries the view that homosexual conduct (sometimes termed sodomy) was sin was thought to have assumed primal form in the archetypal destruction of Sodom as described in the book of Genesis While some recent scholars have questioned this interpretation, in part by emphasizing the primary role of male rape in the offense, the episode gave rise to the expressions "sodomy" and "sodomite," still widely used in that sense.

The classification of homosexuality as a sin was concretized in the early medieval penitentials, which assigned appropriate penalties for various forms of same-sex behavior. It is important to acknowledge, however, that only forbidden acts were punished. Homosexual thoughts or sentiments were not.

Still the act of sodomy itself was regarded as a very serious matter. Traditionally, Catholicism has singled out for special condemnation a group of sins that "cry to heaven" or peccata clamantia: murder, sodomy, oppression of the weak, and defrauding the laborer. The expression goes back to Cain's murder of Abel, whose "blood cries to Heaven" (Genesis 4:10).

In many medieval and early modern jurisdictions, same-sex conduct was judged worthy of death. The practice was commonly termed the peccatum nefandum, the unspeakable sin; and the peccatum contra naturam, the sin against nature.

These terms passed into legal terminology. In his *Commentaries on the English Law,* William Blackstone stated: "What has been here observed, . . . [the fact that the punishment fit the crime] ought to be the more clear in proportion as the crime is the more detestable, may be applied to another offence of a still deeper malignity; the infamous crime against nature committed either with man or beast. A crime which ought to be strictly and impartially proved and then as strictly and impartially punished . . . I will not act so disagreeabl[y] to my readers as well as myself as to dwell any longer upon a subject the very mention of which is a disgrace to human nature. It will be more eligible to imitate in this respect the delicacy of our English law which treats it in its very indictments as a crime not fit to be named; 'peccatum illud horribile, inter christianos non nominandum' [the horrible crime that must not be mentioned among Christians]."

In a number of US states, sodomy was commonly characterized as "the crime against nature."

*Response.* All these ideas are religious in origin. While they may have significance for individuals and the religious organizations to which they belong, they have no binding force in a society that honors the separation of church and state.

# 7  *Homosexuality is the work of the Devil.*

*The Charge.*  No decent person in his right mind would be tempted on his or her own to engage in such an odious practice as sodomy.  Therefore such indulgence must be inspired by the Devil, who tempts his victims to engage in sin.

*Historical Background.*  While many religions acknowledge the maleficent influence of evil spirits, Christianity and Islam are the only faiths to have elevated the Devil to a powerful indvidual status that can compete with that of the Godhead itself.  These religions regard the Devil as a rebellious fallen angel who is tireless in his efforts to tempt human beings to sin.  In Christianity, the Devil has been thought to have a particular affinity with witches, heretics, and other sinners.

This notion that same-sex behavior is the product of diabolic intervention gained credence in the advancing climate of superstition that blighted the closing phases of the Roman Empire.  This is evident in Justinian's punitive Novella [new law] 77, of 538 CE, which excoriates "certain men, seized by diabolical incitement, [who] have abandoned themselves to the basest forms of lasciviousness and engage in practices contrary to nature."

Notions of this kind feed upon two free-floating assumptions.

1) The Devil thrives as a virtually independent power, able to do his will largely unchecked by God or humanity. This concept, generally absent from the Hebrew Bible, probably stems from the migration of Iranian (Zoroastrian) dualism to the West.

2) Paradoxically, homosexuality, while everywhere rejected by decent opinion, seems to exercise an irresistible attraction on those who have been exposed to it. Otherwise inexplicable, such an attraction became more understandable when ascribed to diabolic intervention.

Needless to say, this paradox is rooted in the contradictions of the anti-homosexual polemic itself, and in the well-known fact that tabooed behavior patterns acquire glamor from their very forbidden status.

There are a number of parallels between the medieval witchcraft delusion and the condemnation of sodomy. Both witchcraft and sodomy have been commonly regarded as the work of the Devil.

Few subscribe to a belief in witchcraft today, but same-sex behavior still attracts eccentrics who field the diabolical allegation. Writing on October 27, 2011, Daniel Avila, a lobbyist and spokesperson for the Subcommittee for the Promotion and Defense of Marriage of the U.S. Catholic Conference, asserted that because being gay is not genetic, it must be the work of the Devil. Avila penned the column in the *Boston Pilot*, the newspaper of the Boston Archdiocese. In the column, he claims that because no definite genetic connection can be established for homosexuality, then logically it follows that homosexuality must be the work of the Devil. He holds that whenever natural causes disturb otherwise typical biological development, leading to the personally unchosen beginnings of same-sex attraction, the ultimate responsibility, on a theological level, is and should be imputed to the Evil One, not to God.

The scientific evidence of how same-sex attraction most likely occurs has not satisfied Avila. And so he reaches a strange conclusion which goes somewhat as follows. People of faith must look back to Scripture's account of the angels who rebelled and fell from grace. In their anger against God, these malcontents prowl about the world seeking the ruin of souls. They continue to do all they can to mar distort, and destroy God's handiwork.

*Response.* Today, few people, even religious individuals, subscribe to the antiquated belief in the Devil as a real person. It is a picturesque survival from former times. Relegated to the level of superstition and popular imagery, as seen in the movies, the notion is no longer really viable.

**BIBLIOGRAPHY**. Jeffrey Burton Russell, Lucifer: The Devil in the Middle Ages, Ithaca: Cornell University Press, 1984.

# 8  Homosexuality is equated with heresy.

*The Charge.*  Every society has certain agreed-upon norms.  To depart from them amounts to heresy.

In his contemporary ebook entitled *The Homosexual Heresy*, Dan Montgomery, a theologian and psychologist, warns that Christians today are being held hostage to a homosexual heresy that seeks to cast aside the Bible and Christian orthodoxy that has anchored the church for two thousand years.

*Historical Background.*  Defined as willful and persistent departure from orthodox Christian dogma, heresy forced the church progressively to refine its doctrines and to anathematize deviant theological opinions. At times heretical movements such as Gnosticism, the mystical belief that the elect received a special enlightenment, and Arianism, greatest of the Christological heresies, seemed almost to overshadow the universal church.

From the time of Constantine the Great (d. 337) onward, the church deployed state power to impose uniformity of belief. In both eastern and western halves of the Roman Empire law subjected pertinacious heretics to branding, confiscation of property, exile, and even death. The assumption that the church had the right to call upon the secular power to suppress heresy survived the Empire itself. In the early Middle Ages in the West, few heretics were noticed or prosecuted from the sixth through the tenth century. When prosperity returned after 1000, however, ecclesiastical and secular authorities noted and persecuted heretics who multiplied particularly at first in the reviving cities of southern France and Italy. The iconoclastic controversy of the eighth and ninth centuries nearly destroyed the Byzantine Empire, where such heresies as dualistic Paulicianism flourished continuously.

Modern hypotheses on the causes of heresy were foreign to the churchmen of late antiquity and the Middle Ages, who simply considered heresy the work of the devil. Author after author repeated stereotypical descriptions and denunciations, routinely ascribing such beliefs and practices to later heretics. These clichés fused into a type-figure of the heretic with conventional traits: his pride, since he has dared to reject the teaching of the official Church; his superficial mien of piety, which must be meant to deceive, since he is in fact an enemy of the faith; and his secrecy, contrasted with the teaching of the Church, which is broadcast to the four winds. Most significantly, the heretic is often accused of counterfeiting piety while secretly engaging in libertinism - and the form of sexual libertinism most often imputed to him is homosexuality, or sodomy, as the term generally favored from the end of the twelfth century onward.

Even before the end of antiquity, Western Christian controversialists, using a charge pagans had once leveled against them, had accused members of dissident sects of engaging in unmentionable orgies "for the sake of pleasure." Not satisfied with their promiscuous intercourse with women, some of them, in the words of the Apostle, "were consumed with their lust for one another." A sect called the Levites, after the members of the tribe who officiated in the Temple in Jerusalem, were reported by Epiphanius of Salamis not to have intercourse with women, but only with one another. It was these who were held in distinction and honor by other libertine Gnostics, because they "had sowed no children for the Archon," that is to say, had begotten no offspring whose souls would like theirs be trapped in the lower, material world and could not ascend to heaven. Such charges were also hurled against the Manichaeans, who derived from Zoroastrianism the dualistic doctrine that an evil god created matter and human reproduction in the sense of having more bodies to rule.

It was at the end of the eleventh century that the so-called Bulgarian heresy became known in Western Europe. It was also known as the Albigensian or Cathar heresy. This was a dualistic ideology that had flourished in the kingdom of Bulgaria, which some ascribed to a priest named Bogomil, who combined the beliefs imported from the Byzantine Empire (Paulician and Manichaean) into a new system. From the reign of Tsar Peter (927-969) onward these doctrines were propagated throughout Europe. The Bogomils believed that the Devil was the creator of the visible, material world and that Christ was a phantom who had no ordinary body, was not born of Mary, and did not truly suffer on the cross. They rejected the sacraments, including baptism and the eucharist, in favor of initiation rites that included the laying on of hands, and identified the Devil with the Jewish god, the demiurge whose revelation in the

Hebrew Bible they accordingly repudiated. In their rejection of the Greek Orthodoxy propagated from Byzantium, the heretics were as radical as one could imagine. They subjected the Gospel narratives to a special exegesis that made all the miracle stories symbolic and allegorical.

Since the Bulgarian heresy was the religious deviation par excellence of the later Middle Ages, all heretics in Western Europe came indiscriminately to be labeled bulgari, which became bougres in Old French and buggers in Middle English. But in addition to heresy, the term gained the meanings of sodomite and usurer. It has been asserted that this was only the church's way of defaming unbelievers and provoking hatred for them. In fact, however, they advocated coital abstention because they retained the dualist notion of the wrongfulness of procreation, and may have tolerated sterile promiscuity, at least in the lower ranks of their sect. It is also quite possible that their highest ranks, the so-called perfecti, included more than their share of homosexuals, given the affinity of a certain homosexual character type for leadership in religious communities.

The anti-homosexual doctrines of the Catholic Church, grounded in the prohibitions of the Hebrew Bible which the Cathari rejected, may have added to the alienation of such types from its fold. The oft-repeated allegations of homosexual conduct were not without foundation: a promiscuous sodomite, Arnold de Verniolle of Pamiers, was caught in a heretic hunt in 1323. After careful examination of the evidence most modern historians have concluded that the accusations of debauchery and sodomy against the Cathars had some justification and corresponded to the survival of the mores of pagan Mediterranean antiquity in the folkways of Provence.

The further association of buggery with usury stemmed from the fact that medieval economic doctrine held money to be sterile, so that the earning of interest was equated with "unnatural" non-reproductive forms of sexual expression. But all these factors coalesced to make bougre and bugger  Ketzer and ketter mean not only heretic but also sodomite. German even distinguished the sodomite as the Ketzer nach dem Fleisch, while the heretic proper was the Ketzer nach dem Glauben.

In texts of the thirteenth century, it is true, the general meaning of "heretic" still prevails. Then also, however, scholastic theologians such as Albertus Magnus and Thomas Aquinas defined the "crime against nature by reason of sex" as second only to murder in its heinousness, and the social intolerance of homosexual expression rose to a point where everyone under the authority of the church was obliged to profess heterosexual interests alone. Moreover, the ecclesiastical courts gained the authority to try persons suspected of sodomy, as a crime under canon law, and then to relax them to the civil authorities for execution.

Contrary to the modern belief that the term faggot for "effeminate homosexual" drives from the practice of burning such offenders at the stake, in England the penalty for both sodomy and witchcraft was hanging. As the significance of the Albigensian heresy receded, the meaning bugger equals "sodomite" remained, and in the statute 25 Henry VIII  c.

6 (1533), the word buggery is attested for the first time in English in the unequivocal sexual meaning. In German such terms as Bubenketzer for "pederast" retain the same association of ideas. Some writers even branded sodomy as worse than murder, for the murderer kills only one human being, while the sodomite seeks the death of the entire human race, which would perish if one and all ceased to procreate.

In Cologne Meister Johannes Eckhart (d. 1327) launched a pantheistic mysticism that often became heretical among his Rhenish followers. Partly inspired by the Rhenish mystic, Beguines and Begards, lay groups living communally in celibacy, concentrated in the Flemish towns, were accused of lesbianism more often than of sodomy with males. The general disruption of order by famines, endemic after 1314; the Black Death, which returned every ten years for a century after 1347 and the Hundred Years War - all these factors led to both flagellants and dissipation as well as anti-Jewish outbursts, witch trials, and intensified persecution of sodomites.

Certainly the theological overlap of heresy and sodomy served to intensify the hatred and aversion with which homosexuality was regarded by the masses of the faithful in Western Europe from the late thirteenth century down to modern times. In later medieval law codes heresy and sodomy were both capital crimes, and the accusation of "unnatural vice" was one of the charges brought against the Templars in a series of trials the objective basis of which remains disputed among medieval historians. Again, there is a real possibility that sexual non-conformity was the initial impetus that distanced the heretic from the Church, both then and in later times, when skepticism and unbelief replaced heresy as the chief foes of Christian dogma. It is noteworthy that in Great Britain bugger has, apart from the slightly archaic legal usage, been a taboo word that could not be used in polite company because of the images and emotions which it evoked.

A final consequence of the association of heresy and sodomy was a positive one, in this sense. The criminalization of both came to be seen as expressions of the religious intolerance decried by antitrinitarians in the seventeenth century and by deistic thinkers in the eighteenth. The antithesis of the doctrine of the medieval Church was the conviction that crimes against religion and morality, which included heresy and sodomy par excellence, should not be the object of criminal sanctions unless they harmed third parties or the interests of society in general. It is therefore all the more regrettable that in the English-speaking world - where freedom of conscience and toleration of sectarianism in religion came comparatively early - the place of buggery in the scheme of medieval intolerance was overlooked and the statutes adopted from canon law were perpetuated as bulwarks of morality.

*Response*. In a society such as ours that honors the separation of church and state, the notion of heresy is no longer viable. Even when it was, it was by no means clear that sodomy ranked as a heresy, despite many such assertions over the centuries.

**BIBLIOGRAPHY**. Michael Goodich, The Unmentionable Vice: Homosexuality in the Later Medieval Period, Santa Barbara, CA: ABC-Clio Press, 1979; Malcolm Lambert, Medieval Heresy: Popular Movements from Bogomil to Hus, London: Edward Arnold, 1977.

# 9 *Jesus' Incarnation required the death of the Sodomites.*

*The Charge.* Jesus would not have consented to come into a world tainted by sodomy. Accordingly, the sodomites had to die before he would consent to incarnate.

*Historical Background.* One of the strangest Christian motifs of homonegativity goes back to the thirteenth century, when an Italian prelate Jacobus of Voragine (ca. 1230-1298) compiled a book of edifying Christian stories called the *Legenda Aurea* (the Golden Legend). Section 6 of that book is entitled "The Birth of Our Lord Jesus Christ According to the Flesh." There we encounter the following extraordinary claim: "[a]nd even the sodomites gave witness by being exterminated wherever they were in the world on that night, as Jerome says 'a light rose over them so bright that all who practiced this vice were wiped out; and Christ did this in order that no such uncleanness might be found in the nature he had assumed.' For as Augustine says, God, seeing that a vice contrary to nature was rife in human nature, hesitated to become incarnate." (W. G. Ryan, trans., 1993, p. 41).

No such passage has been found in the authentic writings of Jerome or Augustine, though the claim could have appeared in some texts that are simply ascribed to those early Christian writers. In all likelihood, however, the notion arose in the high Middle Ages, perhaps by some scholastic thinker whom Jacobus purloined.

At all events, this murderous legend enjoyed considerable popularity in Christian Europe during the Middle Ages. For example, the *Flores Temporum* a chronicle of the world's history compiled by a Swabian Franciscan, Hermannus Gigas, records several portents foretelling the coming of Christ, such as the appearance of a spring of olive oil in Rome, the death of all sodomites, and the rising of three suns in the East which merge into one.

The motif recurs in the fifteenth-century Caxton translation of the Golden Legend. "And it happed this nyght, that all the sodomytes that dyde synne ayenst nature were deed and extynct, for god hated so moche this synne, that he myght not suffre that nature humayne whiche he had taken, were delywerd to so grete shame. Wherof saint Austin saith, that it lackyd but lyttl, that god would not become man for that synne."

The notion of the death of the Sodomites on the first Christmas Eve began to fade in the early eighteenth century—but has not yet disappeared entirely. As recently as 2004 a Greek Orthodox priest pronounced that homosexual conduct was very dangerous. The proof was that the sodomites had to die on Christmas Eve for the Incarnation to take place.

***Response.***    Needless to say, history records no such mass extinction of sodomites in or about the year 4 BCE. Despite its longevity, this tale amounts to an urban legend.

# 10 *The colloquial use of the word "faggot" reflects the medieval custom of burning sodomites at the stake.*

***The Charge***. The *Gay Slang Dictionary* offers this definition for the word faggot: "A male homosexual, a term applied to gays during the Inquisition when they were burned along with witches."

In the Middle Ages sodomy was punished by the death penalty, generally through burning at the stake. The word faggot commemorates this harsh practice.

***Background***. One of the most persistent myths that have gained a foothold in the GLBT movement is the belief that "faggot" derives from the basic meaning of "bundle of sticks used to light a fire," with the historical commentary that when witches were burned at the stake, "only presumed male homosexuals were considered low enough to help kindle the fires."

The English word has in fact three forms: faggot, attested by the Oxford English Dictionary from circa 1300; fadge, attested from 1588; and faggald, which the Dictionary of the Older Scottish Tongue first records from 1375. The first and second forms have the additional meaning "fat, slovenly woman" which according to the *English Dialect Dictionary* survived into the nineteenth century in the folk speech of England.

The homosexual sense of the term, unknown in England itself, appears for the first time in America in a vocabulary of criminal slang printed in Portland, Oregon in 1914, with the example "All the fagots (sissies) will be dressed in drag at the ball tonight." The apocopated (clipped) form fag then arose by virtue of the tendency of American colloquial speech to create words of one syllable; the first quotation is from the book by Nels Anderson, *The Hobo* (1923): "Fairies or Fags are men or boys who exploit sex for profit." The short form thus also has no connection with British fag as attested from the nineteenth century (for example, in the novel *Tom Brown's Schooldays*) in the sense of "public school boy who performs menial tasks for an upperclassman."

In American slang faggot/fag usurped the semantic role of bugger in British usage, with its connotations of extreme hostility and contempt bordering on death wishes. In more recent decades it has become the term of abuse par excellence in the mouths of heterosexuals, often just as an insult aimed at another male's alleged want of masculinity or courage, rather than implying a sexual role or orientation.

The ultimate origin of the word is a Germanic term represented by the Norwegian dialect words fagg, "bundle, heap," alongside bagge, "obese, clumsy creature" (chiefly of animals). From the latter are derived such Romance words as French bagasse and Italian bagascia, "prostitute," whence the parallel derivative bagascione whose meaning matches that of American English faggot/fag, while Catalan bagasse-jar signifies "to faggot; to frequent the company of loose women."

In the English common law both witchcraft and buggery were punishable by hanging, not burning. Moreover, in the reign of the homosexual monarch James I the execution of heretics came to an end, so that by the time American English gave the word its new meaning there cannot have been in the popular mind even the faintest remnant of the complex of ideas credited to the term in the contemporary myth. It is purely and simply an Americanism of the twentieth century.

Quite unrelated is the current usage in Britain of the word faggot to describe a kind of meatball.

*Response*. Given the fact that the term faggot cannot refer to burning at the stake, why does the myth continue to enjoy popularity in the gay movement? On the conscious level it serves as a device with which to attack the medieval church, by extension Christianity in toto, and finally all authority. There are better ways to do these things, if need be. On another level, it may linger as a "myth of origins," a kind of collective masochistic ritual that willingly identifies the homosexual as victim.

It should be evident that the word faggot and the ideas that have been mistakenly associated with it serve no useful function; the sooner both are abandoned, the better.

**BIBLIOGRAPHY**. Warren Johansson, "The Etymology of the Word Faggot," Gay Books Bulletin, 6 (1981), 16-18, 33.

# 11 *Homosexuality must never be explicitly mentioned: it is truly unspeakable.*

*The Charge*. In E. M. Forster's novel entitled *Maurice*, the homosexual main character describes himself as follows: "I am an unspeakable of the Oscar Wilde sort."   Rightly so.   In fact some types of behavior are so despicable that they must never be mentioned or discussed.   Same-sex acts are prime examples.   Adhering to a strict policy of abstention is best for all of us.

Indisputably, the text you are reading violates this sound precept.   In the name of all that is decent, you must stop this folly forthwith!

*Historical Background.* Taboos on uttering certain words and phrases thrive in many societies.   However, there is a distinct Western tradition that has proved influential in the context of homonegativity.

The designation of homosexuality as "the nameless sin" reflects the belief that it was unfit even to be mentioned in Christian society.  In 1769, for example, the English jurist Sir William Blackstone described the "crime against nature" as "a subject the very mention of which is a disgrace to human nature. It will be more eligible to imitate in this respect the delicacy of our English law, which treats it in its very indictments, as a crime not fit to be named, peccatum illud horribile, inter Christianos non nominandum." Blackstone alludes not to the statute of 1533, but probably to a single celebrated case, the arraignment of Lord Castlehaven in 1631, where the indictment speaks (in Latin) of "that detestable and abominable sin . . . 'buggery' [in English in the text] not to be named among Christians." (Similar language occurs in a text of Sir Edward Coke, published in 1644.)

Comparable expressions enjoyed the favor of canonists and authors of confessionals on the European continent; in 1700, for example, Ludovico Sinistrari d'Ameno records the terms peccatum mutum ("silent sin"), vitium nefandum ("unspeakable vice"), and vitium innominabile ("unnamable vice"), all designating the crime against nature or sodomy.

A century before, the Andean historian of Peru, Garcilaso de la Vega, claimed that sodomy was so hated by the Incas that the very name was odious to them and they never uttered it. While the Incas were apparently hostile to male homosexuality, Garcilaso's claim that they refused to name it is probably a projection of Christian attitudes. Significantly, Garcilaso also mentions an Amerindian city that, like Sodom, was destroyed by fire for its addiction to homosexual practices.

In late antiquity, through a false etymology based upon the Greek form of the place name, Sodom was interpreted as meaning pecus tacens, "silent herd," a gloss that may have influenced the later formula peccatum mutum. William of Auvergne (ca. 1180-1249) said that it was the "unmentionable vice," noting Gregory the Great's claim that the air itself was corrupted by its mention.

69

Thus it was against an extensive and varied background of usage that Oscar Wilde was to seek to turn the tables in his eloquent plea during his 1895 trial for the "love that dare not speak its name," taking up a phrase from the poem "Two Loves" by Lord Alfred Douglas (1894). In Wilde's statement under cross-examination, the phrase morphed into "a great affection of an elder for a younger Man. It is intellectual... when the elder man has intellect, and the younger man has all the joy, hope and glamour of life before him." In subsequent usage, the phrase "the love that dare not speak its name" became synonymous with homoeroticism in general.

In the New Testament the apostle Paul remarked mysteriously, "For it is a shame even to speak of the things that they do in secret." (Ephesians 5:12). Although this passage has been taken to refer to homosexuality, there is no conclusive evidence to pinpoint the sin (or sins) in question. Nonetheless, the words show that the notion of a transgression too horrible to be named directly was familiar to the early Christians. The Book of Wisdom (14:17) had spoken of "worshipping of idols not to be named."

Latin pagan usage supplies infandus, "unspeakable, abominable" and nefandus, "impious, heinous," both sometimes used of sexual conduct (cf. the later vitium nefandum. In some Spanish texts sodomites are curtly termed nefandarios.

Primitive societies, of course, observe taboos on certain words either because the objects they designate are too dangerous or too numinously sacred to be mentioned outright.

Today many observant Jews prefer not to utter the names for the Godhead as written in Scripture, using "Hashem" (the Name) instead.

In early Christian thought, Dionysius the Areopagite (ca. 500) evolved his negative (or apophatic) theology, which held that God's attributes are too incomprehensible to limited human reason even to be mentioned. Thus by a curious irony, the Christian Trinity and the sodomites are linked in their ineffability/unspeakability.

In today's parlance no such grandiose comparisons seem appropriate. As regards common-garden usage the matter is best understood under the category of euphemism, as seen in the expressions "powder room" for toilet and "go to bed with" for having sex.

Some traditional euphemisms or code words for homosexual include "musical," "sensitive," and "temperamental." Sometimes the avoidance pattern takes the form of deleting any specific word for it, e.g., "Is he. . . ?" "Is she that way?" or "Could he be one?" Everyday usage in other modern languages provides various equivalents for such euphemisms. In French one may speak of "en être" and "comme ça." The expression "ces messieurs" dates from the eighteenth century. With its "so" German is very economical. In Italian we find "così" and "uno di quelli" or with somewhat greater clarity "quel peccato" and "quel vizio." Such expressions can connote either strong distaste for such practices, or a wish to avoid embarrassment (sometimes both). The ultimate in erasure occurs when one merely makes dismissive movements, e.g. displaying a limp wrist for a gay male or performing a stomping gait to indicate a lesbian.

One can find numerous relevant instances of elision and euphemism in twentieth-century fiction, theater, film, and musical lyrics, where oblique references are left as clues but the explicit words are missing. At one time the word "gay" could be used to serve as a code word, but no longer.

In 2004 a popular program appeared on American cable television entitled "The L-Word." In this case everyone knew that the "suppressed" word is "lesbian," so that the show's title itself mocked the censorship tendency.

GLBT people who remain in the closet practice their own form of self-censorship. Unwilling to avow their sexual orientation, they permit their friends and colleagues, most of them at least, to assume that they are conventionally heterosexual. And in fact, many of those who are "out" nonetheless hold that the closet rights of nonadmitters should be respected.

Sometimes this approach even appears in dealing with the dead, especially famous persons, where standard accounts have long shown a tendency to minimalize or ignore the GLBT elements in a person's life. This was formerly the case with biographies of such writers as Walt Whitman. W. Somerset Maugham, and Virginia Woolf. Even now such "degaying" occurs with respect to prominent politicians, diplomats, and religious leaders, who remain enveloped in a discreet cloak of silence. Of course this protection vanishes when they are caught in flagrante and exposed.

Interesting in this connection is the designation MSM (men who have sex with men). This euphemism (if it is that) is said to derive from HIV-prevention groups seeking to reach men who do not regard themselves as having homosexual identities, but who nonetheless engage in same-sex relations. Some of these men may be closeted, others bisexual. For some African Americans the expression "on the down low" performs a somewhat similar function.

*Response*. All knowledge, including that of sexuality, advances through freedom of expression, discussion, and debate. The taboo on the mention of homosexuality violates that imperative. In a lesser way euphemisms also impede proper communication and discussion. Frankness is needed.

The larger issue is one of visibility. For this reason, closeted persons must urged to come out. As always, though this must be a voluntary process.

**BIBLIOGRAPHY**. Michael Goodich, The Unmentionable Vice: Homosexuality in the Later Medieval Period, Santa Barbara, CA: ABC-Clio Press, 1979; Keith Allen and Kate Burridge, Euphemism & Dysphemism: Language Used as Shield and Weapon, New York: Oxford University Press. 1991; idem, Forbidden Words: Taboo and the Censorship of Language, Cambridge: Cambridge University Press, 2006; Ralph Keyes, Euphemania: Our Love Affair with Euphemisms. Boston: Little, Brown and Company, 2010.

# Part II
# Biological Factors

**1** *Even brute animals reject homosexuality. Only human beings, with their limitless capacity for waywardness and perversion, resort to this odious behavior.*

***The Charge.*** Living as they do a life in accordance with nature, animals are incapable of homosexual vice. By contrast, we human beings have become estranged from nature. This estrangement, it is generally agreed, is egregious in the way we abuse the environment. Some of us abuse our bodies too - in ways that Mother Nature never intended. Animals know better.

***Historical Background.*** Adumbrated by Plato in his late dialogue, The Laws, the locus classicus of this claim is Plutarch's essay "Gryllos" (ca. 100 CE), in which an articulate pig asserts the superiority of animal standards of behavior, including sexual conduct. Animals do not, we are told, engage in same-sex behavior.

This general sense of the happy-go-lucky lives of animals has a perennial appeal, as seen even now in television's nature programs. This notion caters to a sentimental hankering for a life without pressure and ambiguity, for a never-never land of bliss, one in which animals supposedly dwell.

The beast criterion is of course selective, since its supporters are unprepared to discard a host of cultural acquisitions and privileges, from clothing and motorized transportation to cell phones and medicines - things not enjoyed by animals. Nor are they inclined (as Aristophanes sardonically pointed out long ago) to perch on roosts at night like fowls or to throw feces as a friendly way of gaining attention as apes are wont to do. The argument, then, rests on a kind of selective amnesia which makes it possible to ignore some aspects of human departure from the animal model, while acknowledging others, if only to deplore them.

At all events the view of animal exemption from homosexuality was by no means universal among the ancient Greeks and Romans. Those times also saw folkloric beliefs, such as the notion that males of the partridge species are so highly sexed that in the absence of females they readily mount each other sexually. Early Christian writers associated the hare with pederasty because of the bizarre notion that it grows a new anus each year. The hyena symbolized gender ambiguity because it ostensibly changed its sex each year. Finally, the weasel, which was supposed to conceive through the mouth, stood for the practice of fellatio. To be on the safe side, the author of the Epistle of Barnabas forbade eating the flesh of any of these creatures.

Over the centuries many preferred to disregard these urban legends of the ancients, colorful as they are, concerning the animal kingdom. Instead a substantial body of learned opinion clung to the idealization that the conduct of animals is exemplary. It serves as a yardstick to determine our "naturalness. This thought complex has been dubbed "animalitarianism" by George Boas, a historian of ideas.

In statements by contemporary anti-homosexual propagandists, it is revealing that they will sometimes first insist that homosexuality must be unnatural, since "even the lowest animals don't do it," and then when confronted with evidence to the contrary exclaim with outrage that same-sex relations drag man down to the subhuman level, "behaving like a filthy swine." Such dodges suggest that moral distinctions develop first. Then this judgmenalism is superimposed on the kingdom of nature, instead of being derived from it in any consistent way.

From time immemorial human beings have favored animal comparisons, both as criticism (dumb as an ox, scared as a rabbit) and as praise (bold as a lion, far-sighted as an eagle). The choice of metaphor depends upon the presuppositions of the speaker. Still, these are all metaphors.

Every species has patterns of sexual behavior unique to itself, so that claiming on supposedly moral grounds that man should imitate the lower animals in their presumed abstention is invalid. Moreover, social control of human sexual activity can only be justified on the grounds that the policy promotes the higher interests of mankind - including the evolutionary progress of the species - rather than following the lead of the instinctual life of creatures far lower on the evolutionary scale.

All living things exist in a world in which - as Darwin showed - they must compete for scarce resources; but while nature confronts scarcity with redundance, man confronts scarcity with foresight. That is to say, lower forms of organic life survive by engendering such myriads of young that at least a minimal number will reach adulthood and the reproductive stage; but humanity survives by economic and demographic measures that seek to proportion his numbers to the resources available for consumption. Especially given the absence of superfetation in the human female, the notion that "homosexuality means race suicide" is preposterous. All human sexual activity, homosexual and heterosexual, occurs in a context of economic and social values that removes it entirely from the genetically programmed coupling of animals, even though such behaviors as competition and courtship anticipate the sexual rivalry and mating of human beings. Finally, the prolonged phase of socializing through which members of human societies must pass - with the need for mentoring and initiation into the world of adulthood - lends a significance to homosexual bonds between adult and adolescent that may find parallels, but no exact equivalents in the social life of animals.

A more recent variation on the old idealization of animals maintains that the principle of animal innocence holds true only among animals in their natural state in the wild. Yet when human beings subject them to special stress, as when they confined together in a small space, aberrant behavior is artificially induced. One might think that any child raised on a farm could refute this myth. It has flourished nonetheless - at least until recently.

Over the last few decades, a body of evidence has been accumulating showing homosexual behavior among many species of animals - behavior that has been observed both in the wild and in captivity. In the 1970s the well-publicized reports of the German ethologist Konrad Lorenz drew attention to male-male pair bonds in greylag geese.

Since Lorenz's time much more data has become available. A massive review published in 1999 by researcher Bruce Bagemihl ascertained that homosexual behavior has been observed in close to 1,500 species, ranging from primates to gut worms, and is well documented for 500 of them. Animal sexual behavior takes many different forms including sex itself, courtship, shows of affection, pair bonding, and parenting among same-sex animal couples.. According to Bagemihl, "the animal kingdom [does] it with much greater sexual diversity" including homosexual, bisexual and nonreproductive sex " than the scientific community and society at large have previously been willing to accept."

Animal homosexual behavior is best known from social species. According to geneticist Simon LeVay, "[a]lthough homosexual behavior is very common in the animal world, it seems to be very uncommon that individual animals have a long-lasting predisposition to engage in such behavior to the exclusion of heterosexual activities. Thus, a homosexual orientation, if one can speak of such thing in animals, seems to be a rarity. One species in which exclusive homosexual orientation occurs, however, is that of domesticated sheep

(Ovis aries). According to the findings, about 10% of rams (males) avoid mating with ewes (females, even though they do mate with other rams."

"Against Nature?" was an exhibition on same-sex behavior in animals organized by the Natural History Museum in Oslo, Norway (September 2006-August 2007). The first exhibition of its kind, it traveled to Bergen, Trondheim, Maastricht, Geneva, and Stockholm.

In fact, the extensive documentation of homosexual behavior in animals seems to offer a telling argument against the traditional view that such conduct constitutes the "sin against nature." Significantly, homosexuality in animals was cited in the United States Supreme Court's 2003 decision in *Lawrence v. Texas*, which struck down the sodomy laws of 14 states.

*Response.* We conclude by summarizing the three stages of knowledge in this realm. First, for centuries it was generally held that, except for a very few aberrant species such as the partridge and the weasel, animals did not engage in homosexual behavior. Then, in recent decades, it was conceded that animals do do it, but only under special conditions of stress. Finally, massive documentation, much of it focused on animals in the wild, has rendered the conclusion inescapable: a full spectrum of homosexual behavior is found among animal species.

**BIBLIOGRAPHY**. Bruce Bagemihl, Biological Exuberance: Animal Homosexuality and Natural Diversity, New York: St. Martin's Press, 1999; Joan Roughgarden, Evolu-

79

tion's Rainbow, Berkeley: University of California Press, 2004; Volker Sommer and Paul J. Vasey, Homosexual Behaviour in Animals: An Evolutionary Perspective, Cambridge: Cambridge University Press, 2006; Aldo Poiani and A. F, Dixon, Animal Homosexuality: A Biosocial Perspective, Cambridge: Cambridge University Press, 2010; Simon LeVay, Gay, Straight, and the Reason Why: The Science of Sexual Orientation, New York: Oxford University Press, 2011.

## 2 Male and female sex organs are shaped to fit one another perfectly, and that is all that one need know.

*The Charge.* Simple observation shows that the sexual organs of the male body protrude, while the female genitalia are concave. The organs fit together like an electrical plug in its socket. For this reason heterosexual couplings are simple, direct, and inviting, while homosexual ones are awkward, contrived, and unsatisfactory.

*Background.* This claim represents a subset of the argument from design. Popular in the seventeenth and eighteenth century, the argument has been revived in recent years by Creationists, who hold that God's imprint is found everywhere in the world in the form of "intelligent design."

In the original concept of the argument from design the world was envisaged as an enormous machine, designed by a supreme watchmaker, with all the parts fitting together perfectly. Voltaire wittily parodied the argument by remarking that clearly the bridge of the nose was designed to accommodate spectacles, while the fjords of Norway were placed there as harbors for ships. Still, if all things were perfectly designed by the Creator at the outset, there would be no need for change over time, and hence no human species, which came about as the result of a long evolutionary process.

Modern sex research has pointed to crucial biological discrepancies that have weakened the old notion of the perfect suitability of male and female sexual organs. For one thing, the "fit" of the penis to the vagina is not notably better than its fit to the anus. Some heterosexual men seem to have in fact a preference for dorsal coitus. Then again, if the penis and vagina were so perfectly matched, other elements would be expected to follow suit. Yet the work of sex clinics, such as the one operated by William H. Masters and Virginia E. Johnson, is largely taken up with issues of sexual dysfunction, such as premature ejaculation. Such problems reveal that everything does not always operate automatically, as one would expect if the male and female anatomies were perfectly engineered to operate in synch. In addition, the male and female biorhythms summoned by sexual excitation show notable differences, and much negotiation and adjustment is required to achieve mutual satisfaction. Heterosexual relations are not, so to speak, as easy as pie. In fact in one respect male-male and female-female relations are superior, since personal experience has given each partner a good sense of what the others needs are likely to be.

In its more sophisticated form, the argument has religious roots. Yet it often survives in ordinary discourse, where the appropriateness of heterosexual coitus is taken for granted.

*Background.* If this argument were conclusive, everyone would experience more pleasure and satisfaction from opposite-sex couplings than same-sex ones. Yet many do not, showing that this coital practice is not a universal rule,

82

As popular language has it, there are different strokes for different folks.

**BIBLIOGRAPHY**. William H. Masters and Virginia E. Johnson, Human Sexual Response, Boston: Little, Brown and Company, 1966; Human Sexual Inadequacy, Boston: Little, Brown and Company, 1970.

# 3  *Homosexuality is pathology, a disease.*

***The Charge.*** For centuries, psychology rightly viewed homosexuality as a form of mental illness. Yet as a result of pressure and intimidation on the part of gay activists, professionals have wavered in this conviction. Instead of steeling themselves in the face of pressure, they lost their nerve. In 1973 the American Psychiatric Association unwisely began the process of declassifying homosexuality as a mental disorder. This retreat cannot change the stubborn fact that this aberrant behavior has always been pathology, and remains such now.

***Historical Background.*** In order to grapple with what is sometimes termed the medical model of homosexuality, some preliminaries are required.

The term neurosis refers to a class of mental disorders involving distress but neither delusions nor hallucinations. This status does not take the neurotic outside the realm socially acceptable norms. As a rule the individual can cope. The term was coined by the Scottish physician William Cullen in 1769 to refer to "disorders of sense and motion" caused by a "general affection of the nervous system."

The contrasting term "psychosis" designates a more radically abnormal condition of the mind, involving a loss of contact with reality In this state, hallucinations and delusions, together with impaired judgment typically occur.

While the two terms, neurosis and psychosis - important in the psychiatric theories of Sigmund Freud - are no longer much used today as diagnostic tools, they have been historically influential.

In that light older approaches were compelled to ask the following question. If homosexuality is in fact a disorder, which is it: neurosis or psychosis? Most advocates of some version of the sickness theory have favored the lesser option of neurosis, because the "sufferer" is usually able to function normally. A few alienists, though, flatly identified homosexuality with psychosis.

Among professionals, the tendency to apply the medical model to same-sex behavior has faded in recent decades. especially after the removal of homosexuality from the list of disorders of the American Psychiatric Association in 1973. Yet the old stereotype still survives in some professional circles, as well as in the folk notion that the "condition" requires a "cure."

In fact, recent years have seen the rise of a dubious procedure called "conversion therapy" (also known as "reparative therapy"). Associated with Christian fundamentalist groups, such interventions have been derided by critics as "pray the gay away." The main organization advocating conversion therapy is the National Association for Research and Therapy of Homosexuality (NARTH); ostensibly secular, this organization often partners with religious groups. Some procedures involve aversive treatments, such as the application of electric shock to the hands and genitals, and nausea-inducing drugs accompanied by homoerotic stimuli; masturbatory reconditioning; visualization; social-skills training; psychoanalytic therapy; and spiritual interventions, such as prayer and group support and pressure. American medical and scientific organizations have expressed concern over conversion therapy and consider it potentially harmful.

Ultimately, the notion that homosexual conduct ("sodomy") is a disorder goes back to the early modern period when the special discipline of forensic medicine emerged, gradually supplanting the role of theologians - with their castigation of the "sin against nature"- in this sphere.

The tradition begins with Paulus Zacchias (1584-1659), a physician at the papal court, who in his *Quaestiones medico-legales* (1621-50) dealt with the forensic evidence for submission to anal sodomy, notably the so-called funnel-shaped anus. His views were parroted by a score of writers down to the last quarter of the nineteenth century.

Over the course of the nineteenth century psychiatry adopted a number of concepts that were for a time to prove crucial for the understanding and classification of homosexuality. The French psychiatrist J. D. E. Esquirol (1772-1840) invented the concept of monomania in 1816 for a specific type of partial insanity in which only one faculty of the mind is diseased. Two main subdivisions of the category were recognized. The first was instinctive monomania, in which only the will is diseased. The second was affective monomania, in which the emotions are excessive or "perverted," and therefore distort behavior. In addition, a quite specific type of the illness was erotic monomania, in which the sexual appetite was diseased and abnormal.

In 1857 Benedict-Auguste Morel (1809-1873) introduced the term degeneration to serve as a vehicle for a complex of religious, anthropological, and pathological assumptions, in particular the belief that acquired defects of the organism can be transmitted to later generations. This innovation led to the psychiatric hypothesis that a range of abnormal mental states could be explained by "degeneration of the central nervous system."

In Germany Ernst von Feuchtersleben (1806-1849), a physician and author, introduced the term psychopathy for "illness of the mind" in general, implying that there could be a pathological state of the mind without a lesion of the brain or central nervous system.

Alongside these contributions, the word perversion had come to be employed in medicine in the sense of "pathological alteration of a function for the worse." Then deviation had in French assumed the meaning of "a departure from the normal functioning of an organ." In England, James Cowles Prichard (1786-1848) coined the expression "moral insanity": "a morbid perversion of the natural feelings,... moral dispositions, and natural impulses, without any remarkable disorder or defect of the intellect or knowing and reasoning faculties, and particularly without any insane illusion or hallucination."

In Germany Johann Ludwig Casper (1796-1864), an expert in forensic medicine, had occasion to examine individuals accused of "pederasty" (= anal intercourse) for the purpose of determining whether their persons revealed that the crime had been committed. In a note appended to a paper of 1833 by the anatomist Robert Froriep, he casually remarked that he had observed a subject in whom sexual desire for the opposite sex was absent - the first such instance to be noted in modern medical literature.

The full-fledged medical concept of homosexuality could not, however, have arisen without the contribution of the pioneer gay scholars Karl Heinrich Ulrichs (1825-1895) and Károly Mária Kertbeny (1824-1882). All the early physicians whose papers introduced "sexual inversion" to the medical world had read the works of one or both of these authors; none arrived at the notion by his own reasoning or by pointed interrogation of a patient with the condition. If they rejected the suggestion that the condition was an idiosyncrasy, a normal variety of the human sexual drive, it was largely because their case material was small and atypical; it usually amounted to one or two individuals examined in prisons or insane asylums. These medical experts were confronted with what was for them an unknown and paradoxical state of mind. The absence of the urge to procreate one's kind, linked with an attraction to members of the same sex with whom coupling could only be sterile, could for the mainstream psychiatrists of that era only be a pathological condition.

It was against the background of these concepts and notions that Carl Friedrich Otto Westphal (1833-1890), Richard von Krafft-Ebing (1840-1902), and Arrigo Tamassia (1849-1917) introduced the concept of die contrre Sexualempfindung (sexual inversion) to psychiatry in articles published between 1869 and 1878. They agreed to define the condition in this way: absence of sexual attraction to members of the opposite sex, with a substitutive attraction to members of one's own sex. The reasoning that underlay their definition was that in normal subjects sexual contact with members of the opposite sex excites pleasure, while with members of the same sex it elicits disgust, but in the cases which they had observed the reverse was true. The condition itself, they concluded, was an "affective monomania," since the rest of the personality of the subject was unaffected.

In 1886 Richard von Krafft-Ebing published the first edition of his celebrated *Psychopathia sexualis*, in which sexual inversion figured in a whole gallery of sexual variations. The author stressed that the sexual act itself, however aberrant it might be, is no proof of the mental abnormality of the person who has committed it, but only that some individuals engage in forbidden sexual acts because they are driven by an involuntary urge.

A long and futile controversy ensued over whether homosexuality deserved to be classified as a "disease." Often the physicians who debated this issue argued that they were taking a sensible middle ground, standing apart from both the religious attitude toward homosexuals as depraved and vicious individuals; and the claims of homosexual apologists that their condition was normal.

In practice, the medical concept of homosexuality as disease was a double-edged sword. On the one hand it served to deny the legitimacy of homosexual expression by labeling the condition pathological; and on the other if offered a ploy to exculpate defendants caught in the toils of the law by labeling them "sick individuals" in need of treatment rather than punishment.

For a long time the psychoanalytic school originated by Sigmund Freud fostered the belief in homosexuality as a mental illness. Psychoanalysts rejected the theory of an innate and unmodifiable condition in favor of a search for its origins in the psychodynamics of the human personality. As a rule the patient universe into which the psychotherapist has delved has not been typical of the overall homosexual population, consisting mainly of subjects with acute moral and legal, if not psychological, problems.

For a good many years, however, Freudian psychoanalysis has been in retreat. By contrast, recent studies by academic psychologists have been able to break out of this vise by producing the experimental or statistical evidence in the wake of Alfred Kinsey to the effect that homosexual subjects were, on standard tests and by a multitude of criteria, indistinguishable from heterosexual ones.

Much of the history of the medicalization of same-sex conduct has to do with psychic characteristics. Yet there is an old tradition that there were also physiological markers. Already, in the seventeenth century Paulus Zacchias had reported that men given to passive sodomy developed funnel-shaped anuses. By the nineteenth century this claim had become commonplace among forensic physicians. It recurs, for example, in the work of the influential Ambroise Tardieu in his *Étude médico-légale sur les attentats aux moeurs* (Paris, 1857). Tardieu also notes features ostensibly found in the penis and the mouth. Of the former organ. he asserts that in the case of active sodomites it becomes long and thin, resembling a dog's member. He also speaks of certain deformations in the mouth of individuals who are given to fellatio.

One must ask whether all these putative cases were common, or simply a projection on the part of the medical examiner who found what he was seeking. This is to say, we may be dealing with urban legends that had very little correspondence to reality. In fact modern medical examinations do not confirm the presence of these physiological deformities.

*Response.* The first major study that challenged the conventional view that homosexuality was intrinsically abnormal summarized the work conducted in the 1950s by the American psychologist Evelyn Hooker. She administered psychological tests on a group of healthy homosexuals and compared those results with results from a control group of heterosexuals. Much to the surprise of the mental-health establishment, skilled psychologists who were adept in making such diagnoses could not distinguish the heterosexuals from the homosexuals on the basis of their test results alone. The test findings indicated that homosexuals were no different from, and had no worse problems than the heterosexuals.

As we have noted, the conventional wisdom at that time was that to be homosexual was to manifest obvious signs of mental disturbance. If this assumption was to be sustained, homosexuals must be shown to be clearly different from the heterosexuals. Yet Evelyn Hooker's study challenged this

91

conventional wisdom. In her study Hooker refuted the generalization that all homosexuals are disturbed.

After a first 1973 effort, in 1980 the American Psychiatric Association finally decided to remove homosexuality per se from its nomenclature of mental illnesses, and in 1986 even the compromise "ego-dystonic homosexuality" was stricken from the list. But the issue lingers among the bitter-enders within the psychiatric profession. Now mostly advanced in years, these individuals resist these changes.

Regrettably, decades of controversy echoed in the mass media have left some members of the general public with the ill-defined belief that "homosexuality is a disease that must be treated." Now, however, this notion is singing its swan song.

**BIBLIOGRAPHY**. Georges Lantéri-Laura, Lecture des perversions: Histoire de leur appropriation médicale, Paris: Masson, 1979; George Chauncey, Jr., From Sexual Inversion to Homosexuality: Medicine and the Changing Conceptualization of Female Deviance, Salmagundi, No. 58-59 (1982-83), 114-46; Gert Hekma, Homoseksualiteit, een medische reputatie: De uitdoktering van de homoseksueel in negentiende-eews Nederland, Amsterdam: SUA, 1987; Vernon A. Rosario, The Erotic Imagination: French Histories of Perversity, New York: Oxford University Press, 1997; Harry Oosterhuis, Stepchildren of Nature: Krafft-Ebing, Psychiatry, and the Making of Sexual Identity, Chicago: Chicago University Press, 2000.

# 4  *Owing to the influence of genes, hormonal factors, and distinctive features of the brain structure, homosexuals stand apart from normals.*

*The Charge.* Biology makes homosexual individuals fundamentally different from normal people. Nothing to be proud of, that idiosyncrasy is a burden these unfortunates must bear without seeking to disguise it.

As the blogger Judson Cox observed in 2004: genetic traits are passed on hereditarily. All that we are is a result of our ancestors. Sex is primarily a biological function designed for procreation. Homosexuality would have to be passed on by recessive genes, like forms of blindness, dwarfism, and retardation. . . . If one claims to be "born gay," one is admitting to be a biological mistake, a freak of nature.

*Background.* Twin and adoption studies suggest that there is in fact a biological component in sexual orientation—though it is certainly not the whole story. Identical (monozygotic) twins are more likely to share the same orientation than fraternal (dyzygotic) twins. This finding holds for both twins raised together and those raised apart, ruling out the possibility that such differences reflect upbringing alone.

Various researchers have posited that certain traits are

characteristic of gay people. Statistically, for example, it is claimed that gay men and lesbians have about a 50 percent greater chance of being left-handed or ambidextrous than straight men or women. The relative lengths of gay-male fingers has also been found to be significant. The index fingers of most straight men are said to be shorter than their ring fingers, Another hypothesis suggests that the hair-whorl patterns on gay heads are more likely to go counter-clockwise than clockwise. It seems, though, that there is not enough evidence to establish any of these assertions.

There are also some more carefully controlled scientific studies. A 1991 study by Simon LeVay and others published in the journal *Science* concluded that the hypothalamus, which controls the release of sex hormones from the pituitary gland, in gay men differs from the hypothalamus in straight men. The third interstitial nucleus of the anterior hypothalamus (INAH3) was found to be more than twice as large in heterosexual men as in homosexual men. This study elicited some criticism because it used brain tissue obtained at autopsies, and all of the homosexual subjects in the study were believed to have died from complications of HIV/AIDS.

A 2001 study showed that HIV status has no significant effect on the INAH3. This study, which also used brain tissue from autopsies, did not reveal any significant difference between the size of the INAH3 in gay men and straight men. It did, however, indicate that in gay men, neurons in the INAH3 are packed more closely together than in straight men.

It has been claimed that chromosome linkage studies of sexual orientation demonstrate the presence of multiple contributing genetic factors throughout the genome. In 1993 Dean Hamer and his colleagues published findings from a linkage analysis of a sample of 76 gay brothers and their families, Hamer et al. found that the gay men had more gay male uncles and cousins on the maternal side of the family than on the paternal side. Gay brothers who showed this maternal pedigree were then tested for X chromosome linkage, using twenty-two markers on the X chromosome to test for similar alleles. In another finding, thirty-three of the forty sibling pairs tested were found to have similar alleles in the distal region of Xq28, which was significantly higher than the expected rates of 50% for fraternal brothers. Somewhat inaccurately, this finding earned the name of the "gay gene" in the media, causing significant controversy. It is unlikely that gay genes as such will be found, but there may be, as this and other studies suggest. chromosomal variations.

Homosexual behavior has been documented among hundreds of animal species. Yet there is little scientific data to show why this should be so. Some studies of rats seemed to show that exposure to sex hormones in the womb during a critical period in brain development affects future sexual orientation. By manipulating hormone levels during this time, scientists can make rats engage in homosexual behavior later on. Many doubt that this finding can be applied to humans.

Research along these lines has encountered resistance in

various quarters. Those who wish to "cure homosexuality" by religious or other intervention object to the idea that a homosexual orientation is conditioned by factors that cannot be changed. In such a perspective, homosexuality might even be regarded as "God-given," horror of horrors. For their part, some gay-friendly observers fear that confirmation of such research might strengthen the stereotype that gay men and lesbian are oddities–what used to be termed "stepchildren of nature." In a worse-case scenario, detection of some markers of this kind might even encourage parents to abort fetuses regarded as likely to become gay.

*Response.* Research of this kind is in its early stages, and some studies seem to be contradicted or modified by others. It is probably fair to predict that, when the research findings are all in, biological factors will be found to inform sexual orientation by providing a disposition or capacity to experience sexual attraction to one sex or the other, or to both. The outcome must be the product of particular life choices in the course of individual development. In other words, both heredity and environment will be seen to play a role.

**BIBLIOGRAPHY**. Simon LeVay, Gay, Straight, and the Reason Why: The Science of Sexual Orientation, New York: Oxford University Press, 2011.

# 5   *In terms of Darwinian evolution, homosexuality makes no sense.*

***The Charge.*** The Darwinian theory of evolution is now generally accepted as the definitive account of the origin and development of life's many varieties, including human life. Yet homosexual behavior is not compatible with this overarching theory. It remains an anomaly.

***Background.*** In the current approach known as evolutionary biology the inclusive fitness of an organism is the sum of its classical fitness (that is, how many of its own offspring it produces and supports) and the number of equivalents of its own offspring it can add to the population by supporting others. Advocates of inclusive fitness theory hold that an organism can improve its overall genetic success by cooperative social behavior.

From the gene's point of view, evolutionary success ultimately depends on leaving behind the maximum number of copies of itself in the population. Until 1964, it was generally believed that genes only achieved this goal by causing the individual to leave the maximum number of viable offspring. However, in 1964 W. D. Hamilton demonstrated mathematically that, because close relatives of an organism share some identical genes, a gene can also increase its evolutionary success by promoting the reproduction and survival of these related or otherwise similar individuals.

How does this principle relate to homosexual behavior? Sexual practices that significantly reduce the frequency of heterosexual intercourse also decrease the chances of successful reproduction, and for this reason, they would appear to be maladaptive in an evolutionary context. At least that would be so with a model that follows a simple Darwinian model of natural selection - on the assumption that homosexuality would reduce this reproductive frequency. Several theories have been advanced to explain this contradiction, and new experimental evidence lends them plausibility.

Some scientists have suggested that homosexuality is adaptive in a non-obvious way. By way of analogy, the allele (a particular version of a gene) which causes sickle-cell anemia when two copies are present may also confer resistance to malaria with a lesser form of anemia when one copy is present (this is called heterozygous advantage).

The so-called "gay uncle" hypothesis posits that people who themselves do not have children may nonetheless increase the prevalence of their family's genes in future generations by providing resources (food, supervision, defense, shelter and the like) to the offspring of their closest relatives. This hypothesis is an extension of the theory of kin selection.

Kin selection was originally developed to explain apparent altruistic acts which seemed to be maladaptive. Proposed by J.B.S. Haldane in 1932, the concept was later elaborated by others, including John Maynard Smith, W. D. Hamilton and Mary Jane West-Eberhard. The concept also served to explain the survival strategies of certain social insects where most of the members are non-reproductive.

Brendan Zietsch of the Queensland Institute of Medical Research has proposed an alternative theory to the effect that men exhibiting female traits become more attractive to females and are thus more likely to mate, provided the genes involved do not drive them to complete rejection of heterosexuality.

In a 2008 study published in the journal *Evolution and Human Behavior* [29 (6): 424-433], its authors stated that "There is considerable evidence that human sexual orientation is genetically influenced, so it is not known how homosexuality, which tends to lower reproductive success, is maintained in the population at a relatively high frequency." They hypothesized that "while genes predisposing to homosexuality reduce homosexuals' reproductive success, they may confer some advantage in heterosexuals who carry them." and their results suggested that "genes predisposing to homosexuality may confer a mating advantage in heterosexuals, which could help explain the evolution and maintenance of homosexuality in the population." However, in the same study, the authors noted that "nongenetic alternative explanations cannot be ruled out" as a reason for the heterosexual in the homosexual-heterosexual twin pair having more partners, specifically citing "social pressure on the other twin to act in a more heterosexual way" (and thus seek out a greater number of sexual partners) as an example of one alternative explanation. Also, the authors of the study acknowledge that a large number of sexual partners may not lead to greater reproductive success, specifically noting there is an "absence of evidence relating the number of sexual partners and actual reproductive success,either in the present or in our evolutionary past."

Significant new evidence on a plausible mechanism for the evolution of "gay genes" has emerged from the work of Andrea Camperio-Ciani and his colleagues. In two large, independent studies they found that the female relatives of homosexual men tended to have significantly more offspring than those of the heterosexual men. Female relatives of the homosexual men on their mother's side tend to have more offspring than those on the father's side. This indicates that females carrying a putative "androphilia genes" complex are more fecund than women lacking this complex of genes, and thereby can compensate for any decreased fertility of the males carrying the genes. This is a well known phenomenon in evolution known as "sexual antagonism," and has been widely documented for many traits that are advantageous in one sex but not in the other. This research provides experimental evidence of how "gay genes" could not only survive but thrive over the course of evolution.

**Response.** While these research findings are suggestive, it is not certain that they truly resolve the Darwinian problem of how exclusive homosexuals can continue to appear over the generations. Of course, it may be that the etiology is simply cultural. If so, though, how is it that homosexuality has appeared independently in so many human groups, not to mention many species of animals? Some puzzles simply remain, at least in the present state of knowledge.

100

**BIBLIOGRAPHY**. James D. Weinrich, Sexual Land-scapes, New York: Charles Scribner's Sons, 1987; Michael Ruse, Homosexuality: A Philosophical Inquiry, Oxford: Blackwell, 1988; Andrea Camperio-Ciani, F. Corna, and C. Capiluppi, "Evidence for Maternally Inherited Factors Favouring Male Homosexuality and Promoting Female Fecundity," Proceedings of the Royal Society, London B, vol. 271, no. 1554 (Nov. 7, 2004), 2217-21.

# 6   *Homosexuals are biological degenerates.*

*The Charge.* Degeneracy takes many forms, including necrophilia, incest, pedophilia, bestiality, and serial murder. Yet homosexual degenerates seem to be the only such group to have the effrontery to insist that their perversion be accepted as somehow "normal." This appalling demand must be firmly resisted.

As Peter Watson, a young Australian politician, remarked in 2012: "Yes, I am homophobic. Homosexuals disgust me with their decadent attitudes to life and their life styles. They are really bad for our society and they need to be dealt with by the powers to be. The homosexuals are the true social degenerates."

*Historical Background.* The idea of degeneration is related to the idea of decline, Yet instead of emphasizing the historical and cultural factors that were thought to spell civilizational decline, the concept of degeneration has focused on biological determinants that ostensibly decree the deterioration of the human organism. The unfortunates who were subject to this process were termed "degenerates" at the height of the idea's popularity. In the later decades of the nineteenth century, such deviant figures as the alcoholic, the criminal, the nymphomaniac, and the homosexual were stigmatized as degenerates. Thus degeneracy was an umbrella concept, yet one in which same-sex behavior always occupied an important place.

The scientific or pseudo-scientific underpinnings of the concept are summed up in the theory of devolution. Devolution or backward evolution is the notion that a species can change into a more rudimentary form over time. The notion presumes that there is a preferred hierarchy of structure and function, and that evolution must mean progress to more advanced organisms. This may include the idea that some modern species that have lost functions or complexity must be degenerate forms of their full-fledged ancestors.

Broadly speaking, the idea of devolution rests upon the assumption that evolution requires some sort of purposeful development towards "increasing complexity." Yet modern evolutionary theory requires no such presumption, and the concept of evolutionary change is independent of either any increase in complexity of organisms sharing a gene pool.

The concept of devolution or degenerative evolution enjoyed its heyday in the nineteenth century, when many biologists believed that evolution exhibited some kind of direction. One of the first biologists to suggest devolution was the Englishman Ray Lankester, who explored the possibility that evolution by natural selection may in some cases lead to devolution, an example he studied was the regressions in the life cycle of sea squirts. Lankester presented his ideas of devolution in his book *Degeneration: A Chapter in Darwinism* (1880). He was a critic of progressive evolution, pointing out that higher forms existed in the past which have since degenerated into simpler forms. Lankester argued that "if it was possible to evolve, it was also possible to devolve, and that complex organisms could devolve into simpler forms or animals."

The latter decades of the nineteenth century saw a growing fear of degeneration sweeping across Europe creating, it was thought, disorders that led to poverty, alcoholism, moral perversion, and political unrest. The discourse of degeneration raised the possibility that Europe might be perversely nourishing a class of degenerate individuals whose very marginality caused them to be in open revolt against established social norms. This anxiety fostered support for a strong state which ride herd on degenerates, identifying them and segregating them from the rest of the population.

In the 1850s, a French physician B.A. Morel strongly maintained that certain groups of people were degenerating, going backwards in terms of evolution, so that each generation became weaker and weaker. Morel's thinking relied on pre-Darwinian ideas of evolution, especially those of Jean-Baptiste Lamarck, who held that acquired characteristics such as drug abuse and sexual perversions could be passed on to succeeding generations.

Working in the 1880s, the Italian criminologist Cesare Lombroso believed he found clear evidence of degeneration in studying the corpses of criminals. After completing an autopsy on one murderer he found an indentation where the spine meets the neck which he interpreted as a sign of degeneration and subsequent criminality. He also maintained that criminal types could be identified by a particular configuration of the feet.

During the twentieth century the growing panic about

degeneration served to rationalize various eugenic programs in Europe and the United States - to terrible effect. These programs involved the sterilization of those who were supposedly unfit to reproduce. For their part, the Nazis took up these eugenic efforts, seeking to exterminate all those who might corrupt future generations.

In 1892 the Hungarian journalist Max Nordau published a book entitled *Entartung* (rendered in English as *Degeneration*) that was widely influential for a time. Nordau blamed modern social phenomena for creating pathological conditions under which unacceptable art was produced. The writers and artists who created such work he diagnosed as "degenerate." Nordau even produced photographs of such figures as Baudelaire and Verlaine with the implication that their very appearance revealed their fallen state.

The Nazis applied the concept of degeneration to the aesthetic sphere, banning "degenerate" (entartete) art and music. By 1937 the concept of degeneracy was firmly entrenched in Nazi policy. On June 30 of that year Josef Goebbels put Adolf Ziegler, the head of the Reichskammer der Bildenden Künste (Reich Chamber of Visual Art), in charge of a six-man commission authorized to confiscate from museums and art collections throughout the Reich any art works deemed ultramodern, degenerate, or subversive.

In a series of rapid campaigns some 5,000 works were seized, including 1,052 by Emil Nolde, 759 by Ernst Heckel, 639 by Ernst Ludwig Kirchner, and 508 by Max Beckmann, as well as smaller numbers of works by other artists, including Ensor, Matisse, Picasso, and Van Gogh. The Entartete

Kunst exhibit offered a selection of these, featuring over 650 paintings, sculptures, prints, and books from the collections of thirty-two German museums. The exhibition of these works was intended to incite further revulsion against the "perverse Jewish spirit" ostensibly penetrating German culture It opened in Munich on July 19, 1937 and remained on view until November 30 before traveling to eleven other cities in Germany and Austria.

In the early twenty-first century one might have thought that the discourse of degeneration was completely passé, at least in respectable circles. Yet it is not, or not quite. In 2012 the British economic historian Niall Ferguson published a book entitled *The Great Degeneration.* Alarmingly, he detects the symptoms of decline all around us today: "slowing growth, crushing debts, aging populations, antisocial behavior. How has Western civilization gone astray?" The answer, Ferguson maintains, is that "our institutions - the intricate frameworks within which a society can flourish or fail - are degenerating. Representative government, the free market, the rule of law and civil society: these were once the four pillars of Western European and North American societies."

Degeneration is occurring, it seems, but not degenerates. That is perhaps an advance, at least rhetorically. Not many, though, would agree with the British historian's pessimistic diagnosis of the state of our civilization.

*Response.* The science underlying the concept of degeneration has always been dubious. The Nazi espousal further tainted the notion. In consequence, the expressions "degeneration" and "degenerate" are rarely encountered these days (the example of Niall Ferguson is a partial exception).

Popular culture supplies another recent instance, though not a very significant one. In a play on words, homophobes decry Ellen DeGeneres, the popular lesbian comedian and celebrity (prominent from 1994, when she received her first television show), by dubbing her "Ellen Degenerate." Whimsically cited by her admirers, this persiflage doesn't cut the mustard.

**BIBLIOGRAPHY**. J. Edward Chamberlain and Sander L. Gilman, eds., Degeneration: The Dark Side of Progress, New York: Columbia University Press, 1985; Daniel Pick, Faces of Degeneration: A European Disorder, c. 1848-c. 1918, Cambridge: Cambridge University Press, 1989.

# Part III
# Social Factors

## 1  *Homosexuality is against the law.*

*The Charge.* Anti-homosexual legislation has long been a hallmark distinguishing civilization from barbarism. These laws are not based on caprice or established by accident but rank as an essential part of mankind's perennial quest to uphold our social decencies.

The law is called upon not simply to prohibit but to foster and encourage as well, inculcating good morals. This proactive approach serves as an indispensable guide in our society because it provides an irrefutable framework within which we can all work, especially in times of confusion or tumult. In Britain Lord Patrick Devlin has forcefully argued that popular morality must influence lawmaking, and that even private acts should be subject to legal sanction if the "reasonable man" finds them unacceptable.

These prohibitions are in accord with natural law; and sodomy, as the apostle Paul instructs us (Romans 1:26-27), is clearly against nature.

When the innate wisdom that resides in these salutary laws is overturned - as has happened in some politically mercurial countries of late - the outcome is dysfunctional to the society. This dismantling of much-needed legislation stems from the machinations of the vociferous gay lobby.

Of long-standing utility, these efficacious provisions must be retained - and restored where necessary.

*Historical Background.* Historically, legal sanctions against homosexual conduct have been linked to the condemnation of sodomy, a broad category that includes oral sex, anal sex, and bestiality. Revealingly, such laws have rarely been enforced against heterosexual couples. In the West the adoption of such legislation has often reflected the sexual ethics of Christianity. Eventually, the prohibitions have made their way into many secular legal codes, even in some non-Christian nations. As a result, sodomy laws are found in much of the world. Today, consensual same-sex acts between adults are illegal in some 70 out of the 195 countries of the world (approximately 36%). In some forty of these male-male sex is targeted exclusively.

A brief historical review, starting with the Roman Empire, will be helpful. Setting aside the murky details of the Lex Scantinia from Republican times, it was with the dynasty of Constantine the Great (305-337) that the first statutes penalizing male homosexuality enter the Roman law codes. Victorious Christianity had ratified the code of sexual morality embodied in Leviticus 18 and made it part of its own constitution. Even so, the first legal texts are couched in the language of Roman virtue and of condemnation of men who "have changed their sex" rather than that of the Latin renderings of the Hebrew Bible.

It is with the Byzantine Emperor Justinian (527-565)

that allusions to the destruction of Sodom enter the logic of Novellae 77 and 141, which prohibit the crime that had caused "whole cities to be destroyed together with their inhabitants." Since the Corpus Juris Civilis became the foundation of legal thinking in Western Europe, these texts were the motivation for the criminalization of sodomy through later centuries.

With the collapse of the Roman Empire, its codes were replaced by barbarian legal traditions that knew little of homosexual behavior as a crime. It was in Canon Law that the religious condemnation of homosexual expression was perpetuated and made a part of popular morality. Nonetheless, centuries of indoctrination were needed to instill the belief in the mass mind that sodomy was a "crime against nature" and the sodomite a criminal on a par with heretics and witches.

The full force of the church's teaching arrived only in the thirteenth century, when the scholastic theologians Albertus Magnus and Thomas Aquinas taught that sodomy was a crime against the order of nature because it denied the procreative function of sexuality, and held it second only to murder in gravity. The close of that century saw not merely legal enactments prescribing the death penalty, but also records of capital punishment. Although executions were never numerous, they served to impress upon the popular mind the horror of "unnatural" sexual conduct. The defamation of sodomy also offered a convenient alibi to the church whenever any misfortune struck, since there was always a reservoir of unpunished sexual immorality within the community. Divine wrath at these unexpiated sins became the explanation, and the "sodomite" served as the scapegoat upon whose head all the ills of society could be blamed.

In England king Henry VIII introduced the first legislation under English criminal law with the Buggery Act of 1533. This law only published sodomy among males, though some offshoot legislation, as in the American colonies and states punished lesbianism as well.

From the end of the thirteenth century until the close of the eighteenth the homosexual was everywhere in Western Europe a criminal and an outcast who had to hide his sexual activity and identity from a persecuting Christian society. With the Enlightenment the legal thinkers of Western Europe began the secularization of the criminal law. Beccaria, Voltaire, and their followers, arguing that the crime of sodomy belonged to canon and not to civil law, convinced the educated public that offenses against religion and morality were matters for confession and expiation rather than concerns of the state. It was against the background of these beliefs that the penal code adopted by the Constituent Assembly of Revolutionary France in 1791 for the first time in modern history omitted the crime of sodomy from the list of punishable offenses, and the Code Napoleon of 1810 retained this innovation. Following the French example, a large number of countries, mainly Roman Catholic ones, reformed their own penal codes in the course of the nineteenth century. In other legal systems, however, the sole change was to replace the death penalty with life imprisonment or some other punishment that fell just short of it.

The recommendations of the Wolfenden Report in England (1957) asserted that "homosexual behaviour between consenting adults in private should no longer be a criminal offence." Following suit, many western governments, including the United States, have repealed their laws targeting homosexual conduct. In June 2003, the United States Supreme Court ruled in Lawrence v. Texas that state laws criminalizing private, non-commercial sexual activity between consenting adults at home on the grounds of morality are unconstitutional since there is insufficient justification for intruding into people's liberty and privacy.

As of 2011, sodomy laws had been repealed or judicially struck down in all of Europe, North America, and South America, except for Antigua and Barbuda, Barbados, Belize, Dominica, Grenada, Guyana, Jamaica, Saint Kitts and Nevis, Saint Lucia, Saint Vincent and the Grenadines, and Trinidad and Tobago. Sodomy remains a serious crime in these countries and in many other parts of the world.

If Christianity is the ultimate source of anti-homosexual legislation in the West, these laws have another root in Muslim-majority countries. In practice Islamic Sharia law stems from both the Qur'an and hadiths. The Qur'anic condemnation of homosexuality was naturally adopted by Muhammad's successors. According to report, Abu Bakr had a wall thrown down upon suspected sodomites, a punishment that is being replicated in the Middle East today. Ali, the fourth caliph, had sodomites burned.

Islamic legal scholars expanded upon the principles they detected in the Qur'an and the hadiths. In this tradition homosexual conduct is not only a sin, but a "crime against God." There are some differences in interpretation among the four mainstream legal schools, but they all agree that homosexual behavior must be severely sanctioned.

What then of the seemingly flourishing pederastic subculture of the Islamic Middle Ages? Is this simply a myth? No it is not, but the phenomenon is mainly a matter of particular sectors, often those that stand apart from the Sunni mainstream. More generally, the de facto toleration of pederasty is linked to the Islamic tendency to the seclusion of women, leading to their removal from public life. In Islam adult-adult male homosexuality has never been tolerated.

Today, in such Muslim-majority countries as Iran, Mauritania, Saudi Arabia, North Sudan, and Yemen, homosexual behavior is punished by the death penalty. In parts of Nigeria and Somalia, the death penalty also prevails.

*Response*. As we have seen in the above historical review, the sodomy laws do not reflect some universal impulse, found in all times and places. Instead they are culturally and historically contingent, generally revealing the influence of Christianity and Islam. Even though sodomy laws are widespread in several parts of the world today, they are generally absent from areas untouched by those two religious traditions.

As far as natural law is concerned, there is no clear consensus as to what its provisions are with regard to sexual behavior, and hence no valid way of using its dictates either to support or annul the sodomy laws.

113

These laws are not on a par with those that condemn murder and theft because they sanction victimless crimes. When consent is present, no one is harmed. Sodomy laws bring no clear benefit to society, and much harm to those subject to them. They limit human happiness, and should be abolished everywhere.

**BIBLIOGRAPHY**. William Eskridge, Jr., Gaylaw: Challenging the Apartheid of the Closet, Cambridge, MA: Harvard University Press, 1999; Dale Carpenter, Flagrant Conduct: The Story of Lawrence v. Texas: How a Bedroom Arrest Decriminalized Gay Americans, New York: W. W. Norton, 2012.

## 2   *Homosexuals have long gravitated to the criminal underworld, with its easy access to alcohol and drugs.*

***The Charge.*** Same-sex acts have traditionally been subject to legal sanction, and rightly so. Cavalier yet closeted, expectant yet withholding, these reprobates are always true to form. Is it surprising that their infamous skill set allows them to consort so readily with the denizens of the criminal underworld?

Their wayward arrogance and pitiful longing for acceptance by other lawbreakers should cause alarm in each and every one of us, upright citizens dedicated to upholding the rules of a civilized society. At present, homosexuals are the one demographic group whose involvement in the drug and pornography industries is disproportionately high. This affinity alone has made homosexuals not only subversive but just plain untrustworthy.

***Historical Background.*** Historically, there have been several reasons for this link between homosexuality and criminality. First, both groups have been forced to live and socialize in rundown quarters of major cities. Sometimes these slum districts were glamorized as "bohemias," but they remained zones of deposit for society's rejects. Moreover, struggling to get by somehow in the face of their stigma, the outgroups have sought solace in alcohol and other stimulants. Finally, for their part, homosexual individuals have generally found that survival required them to become well-versed in the arts of concealment. As the blogger Andrew Sullivan has noted: "[W]hen you know you are different, especially in your teens, you keep very careful tabs on what is regarded as "normal." You become obsessed with giving nothing away. You have to develop much sharper skills of human observation, and learn how to mimic what comes easily to others. . . . The art of mimesis comes early - as part of self-defense." (The Dish, January 23, 2013). This capacity for dissimulation, for appearing to be what one is not, has proved a valuable resource in various walks of life, including acting, espionage, and criminal activity.

The best documentation of the link between sexual variation and crime stems from major urban centers. To illustrate this point, three sites of this multinational phenomenon suffice: Florence, London, and New York.

Among Italian cities it was Florence that historically enjoyed the dubious reputation of being excessively "tolerant" of homosexual conduct. This renown is attested by the Middle High German verb florenzen, "to sodomize." And St. Bernardino of Siena (1380-1444), preaching on May 23, 1425 against sodomy, lamented that "You cannot leave Tuscany without being reproached twelve times a day that here we never punish such a vice."

In reality Florentine laws (beginning with that of 1325) severely punished sodomy, but in practice the authorities imposed the death penalty reluctantly, preferring fines or corporal punishments of other types (including castration).

Capital punishment was reserved for cases of special gravity, such as rape, seduction of a small child, or public scandal.

Florence had a special court, that of the Uffiziali di Notte (the "Officers of the Night"), which was charged with the task of monitoring and punishing homosexual acts. Research shows that most of the penalties exacted were fines. The relative mildness of Florentine justice helped to assure the denunciation of notorious sodomites, since the accuser knew that he was unlikely to cause a person's death.

In this way one can see how in "tolerant" Florence the accusations amounted to several thousand. Thanks to this option of mild, but systematic repression (instead of severe, but sporadic), Florentine society succeeded in keeping homosexual behavior under control, despite the existence of a popular culture that treated it indulgently, especially if the culprits were adolescents. Among the names of famous persons accused of sodomy under this system were the artists Leonardo da Vinci, Sandro Botticelli, and Benvenuto Cellini (who was twice condemned).

The existence of a real subculture, and not simply of isolated acts, is confirmed by numerous sermons preached by the above-mentioned Bernardino of Siena in the years 1424-27. In these texts Bernardino mentions various privileged places where sodomites met, especially taverns and pastry shops, noting the hours of the night preferred by the sodomites, those "wild pigs," in their search for sexual partners.

Niccoló Machiavelli, in a letter of February 25,1514, to

his friend Francesco Vettori, amused himself by recalling street by street the path of a common friend in nocturnal quest of boys. Among the locales noted are Borgo Santo Apostolo, Calimala Francesca, and II Tetto de' Pisani.

The prevailing pattern of this subculture resembles that known for other Italian cities of the period: the sodomite couple consists of an adult, who takes the role of the insertor, and an adolescent, who is the insertee. The availability of adolescents for prostitution was decisive for maintaining the subculture; Michael Rocke has calculated that in the period ca.1478-83 ten percent of all Florentine boys had to appear before the authorities charged with sodomy. The same author notes also that those accused of sodomy included a conspicuous number of bachelors and recidivists, whom it is probably accurate to describe as having a "deviant lifestyle."

London presents a number of revealing glimpses over the centuries.

Richard of Devizes' *Chronicle of the Times of King Richard the First* includes an account of the underworld subcultures of London in 1192 that mentions four classes of individuals who certainly (or probably) engaged in homosexual activity: glabriones, "smooth-cheeked, pretty, effeminate boys," pusiones, "little hustlers, kept boys,"molles, "effeminates," mascularii, "man-lovers," a term found only in this passage in all of Medieval Latin, through plainly deriving from the masculorum concubitores of 1 Corinthians 6:9. Thus even in the early Plantagenet period London had its erotic subculture frequented by those who ignored or de-

118

fied the official norms of the Church in the sphere of sexual morality.

The social reality of Elizabethan drama, so much celebrated nowadays, flourished in its own milieu of social marginality. The theaters at which the plays of Marlowe, Shakespeare, and the lesser dramatists of that time were performed had all-male casts, and by tradition the roles of women were taken by boys, so that an ambiance of sexual ambiguity and double-entendre hung over an institution that was constantly assailed for "immorality." Christopher Marlowe ended up being murdered in a tavern brawl.

In England the civil war and the Commonwealth were followed by the Restoration, during which the first signs of a modern homosexual subculture emerge. The social stratification and anonymity of the metropolis facilitated the growth of a clandestine network of meeting places for individuals with unconventional desires. Restoration drama, the novels of Henry Fielding and John Cleland, and the prints of William Hogarth have given the London of that era a reputation for sensuality and excess that contrasted with the sober life of the English countryside. In the late 1720s London was scandalized by the discovery of homosexual clubs, molly houses, in which some men would don women's clothing and even go through mock marriages.

Although burning at the stake was never the penalty for buggery in England, a fate in some ways even worse lay in wait for the convicted sodomite. Such culprits were exposed in the pillory to abuse and assaults of the mob, which could freely pelt the guilty parties with filth and missiles of every

119

kind. The belief that Sodom and Gomorrah had been destroyed because of the sexual depravity of their inhabitants justified these cruel penalties in the eyes of the populace. The Napoleonic wars saw a renewed outburst of intolerance, which resulted in numerous prosecutions. In 1810 a homosexual rendezvous on Vere Street in London was raided by the police, and nine men were subsequently convicted and placed in the pillory, where the commons vented their wrath on them in a manner that bespoke the intensity of popular hatred for those guilty of "unnatural crimes."

Nonetheless, homosexual life persisted beneath the surface of London's commercial and industrial life and the Victorian respectability of the capital of a great empire "on which the sun never set." Homosexuals of the upper social strata rubbed shoulders with hustlers from the depths of the criminal underworld, a phenomenon so aberrant from the standpoint of a class society that as late as the middle of the twentieth century the police could be moved to an investigation merely by evidence of associations of this kind. In 1889 a scandal occurred in which a house in Cleveland Street was discovered to be a place of assignation for homosexual clients and telegraph boys who served them as prostitutes. Oscar Wilde's ruin was also caused by his involvement with this criminal milieu when it was revealed by his archenemy, the Marquess of Queensbury, in 1895.

Since US cities emerged more recently, they were slower to develop the kind of demimonde in which reproved sexual behavior flourished. Towards the end of the nineteenth century, though, New York City harbored a vibrant bohemian and entertainment subculture. As a result of vice investigations of the 1890s, we know of such establishments as the Golden Rule Pleasure Club, Manilla Hall, Paresis Hall, The Palm, the Black Rabbit, Little Bucks, and the Artistic Club. Some of these locales were essentially male brothels, while others offered drinks and entertainment. In the Bowery and lower Broadway areas, the streets were patrolled by aggressive male hustlers, identifiable by their painted faces and red ties.

The first two decades of the twentieth century were the original heyday of Greenwich Village as a cultural center and also as a place of some toleration for lesbians and gay men. Others frequented the nightspots in Harlem, a district which was also the scene of a major black intellectual movement with several significant gay and bisexual participants: the Harlem Renaissance. At this time the modem gay-bar and bathhouse culture began to take shape.

For the bars in New York City and elsewhere in the United States, however, Prohibition (1919-1933) meant devastation, though some of these bars continued as speakeasies. An unintended consequence of the legal change was to make gay and straight bars more similar, since both were now invested with the same atmosphere of clandestinity. After the gay bars reopened, however, many fell under the control of organized crime, which coordinated payoffs to the police. Today some gay bars and other gathering places serve as markets for purchasing drugs. It is not clear, however, that this predilection for controlled substances is greater than in the rest of the population.

Is quantification possible? A forty-eight page study published in the journal *Psychological Reports* in 2005 analyzes some data compiled in 1996 by the Center for Disease Control (CDC), which seem to suggest that US homosexuals are more likely to engage in illegal and socially dangerous behavior than heterosexuals. According to the study, homosexuals are over 107% more likely to have been booked for illegal activity than heterosexuals. However, the report was penned by Dr. Paul Cameron of the Family Research Institute, an organization whose scholarly bona fides has been questioned. In fact, there are no reliable data to this effect because no one knows what the statistical universe (the total number) of GLBT people in the United States is.

*Response.* Why has this marginal status with its criminal taint continued to trouble GLBT people? Over the centuries, the main reason is the opprobrium and illegality that have been imposed upon them in Western society. As this mantle of oppression is being lifted the marginality may be expected to diminish.

Even if–and it is a big if–gay criminality today were to be found to exceed that of the rest of the population that finding would be no more reason for discrimination than it is for certain ethnic groups that have historically had significantly high crime rates.

**BIBLIOGRAPHY**. Rictor Norton, Mother Clap's Molly House: The Gay Subculture in England, 1700-1830, London: GMP, 1992; George Chauncey, Jr., Gay New York: Gender, Urban Culture, and the Makings of the Gay Male World, 1890-1940. New York: Basic Books, 1994; Michael

Rocke, Forbidden Friendships: Homosexuality and Male Culture in Renaissance Florence, New York: Oxford University Press 1996; David Higgs, ed., Queer Sites: Gay Urban Histories Since 1600, London: Routledge, 1999; Matt Cook, London and the Culture of Homosexuality, 1885-1914, Cambridge: Cambridge University Press, 2008.

# 3 Tolerating homosexuality spells decadence, the decline of civilization.

**The Charge.** History has clearly and consistently shown that fatuous toleration of homosexual misconduct weakens a society's moral fabric. Once this process of decay begins it is, all too often, inexorable. The histories of ancient Greece, the Roman Empire, and modern France were all blighted in this way.

Sally Kern, a Republican lawmaker in Oklahoma, put it this way in March 2008: "Studies show that no society that has totally embraced homosexuality has lasted more than, you know, a few decades. So it's the death knell of this country. I honestly think it's the biggest threat our nation has, even more so than terrorism or Islam – which I think is a big threat. . [Because] what's happening now is they are going after, in schools, two-year olds. . . And this stuff is deadly, and it's spreading, and it will destroy our young people; it will destroy this nation."

In America today the social media - led by the Internet - have greatly increased access to pornography which has become a fact of daily life. These electronic media also facilitate lewd "sexting" messages and promote hookups - casual short-term arrangements where commitment, quite simply put, ranks as a bizarre anachronism.

Degenerates of all kinds thrive in this permissive setting.

For their part, movies and television relentlessly promote the homosexual lifestyle. The abomination of "gay marriage" is not only accepted, but celebrated. Sapping unit cohesion, open gay men and lesbians are now welcome in the military. This misplaced tolerance places our national security is in peril.

Andrew Sullivan, an openly gay political commentator, cheekily proclaims that homosexuality has become "virtually normal."

In this way we are teaching future generations that there is no merit in conforming to the rules of virtuous living. Supplanting the dedication that decency requires, we have the cult of instant gratification, a sure road to perdition.

Similar (often identical) problems are plaguing Europe as well. In fact the situation there is even worse owing primarily to demographics. The great disaster - and worse still, sad fate - in combining homosexuality and hedonism is that Europeans are simply not reproducing.

***Historical Background.*** Fears of historical decline are long-standing and recurrent. This propensity is probably rooted in the psychological fact that, in growing older, we human beings tend to view earlier phases of our lives through rose-colored glasses, deprecating the present moment in favor of our idealized salad days.

Projected onto peoples and societies, this perspective suggests that the "good old days" were better than the present, while the future is likely to be still worse. In some conservative thinking this comparison enjoys the status of an archetypal pattern. Woe is us!

The sources of this mode of complaining lie far in the past. As has often occurred in the history of ideas, classical thought is foundational.

The Greeks and Romans entertained two chief models of epochal decline. According to the first, as outlined by the seventh-century poet Hesiod, human society began in an Edenic time of harmony and abundance, termed the Golden Age. In due course, however, this utopia yielded in turn to Silver and Bronze Ages of increasing barbarism - until society sank into the bleakness of the final Iron Age.

This pessimistic historical scheme paints a grim picture. The pattern is much like the seasons changing on their relentless passage to winter, and the human body's successive stages of decline, The only consolation lies the happy memories associated with the Golden Age.

All was not lost, though, at least not necessarily. According to some poets like Vergil and Horace, who flourished in the entourage of the emperor Augustus (ruled 27 BCE-14 CE), this age of bliss could return, starting the cycle anew.

The other model of decline idealizes a rural past with a low level of technology, when society was happy precisely because of scarcity. Since there was little to steal, theft was rare. Moreover, in the prevailing minimalist circumstances, those who had afforded themselves and their family members some scanty prized possessions guarded them carefully.

Hardship caused people to work together instead of against each other. "Sweet are the uses of adversity," as Shakespeare was later to put it.

A variation was the ploy of locating primitive virtue not in the remote past but in contemporary tribal societies. Tacitus lauded German uprightness, condemning in contrast Roman decadence, luxury, covetousness, and self-indulgence. Revealingly, not until the Christian Salvian, who wrote during the collapse of the Empire in the fifth century, does homosexual conduct per se figure in the catalog of vices.

With the adoption of Christianity in the fourth century, Eusebius and other Patristic writers elaborated a new concept of progress, that of advancing states of moral perfection. Thus in ancient Israel polygamy and even under certain circumstances incest (Lot and his daughters) had been permissible.

A great signpost on this road of human moral advance was the Incarnation of Christ, which would lead in due course to the Second Coming and the restoration of all things. Before the longed-for consummation could be secured, however, there would be a period of frightful apocalyptic turmoil. Even though the Christian vision was on the whole more optimistic than previous ones, ironically the looming danger of sudden reversal - of decline after progress - was to prove a haunting, prophetic vision.

The victory of the Moderns in their quarrel with the Ancients in late seventeenth-century France, as well as the

127

scientific revolution consummated at the same time in the work of Sir Isaac Newton, prepared the way for the Enlightenment belief in human progress through science and institutional reform for a mankind that was basically good. "Decline" seemed to be in decline.

The publication of Charles Darwin's *Origin of Species* in 1859 set the doctrine of evolution on its triumphant march, seeming to demonstrate scientifically and conclusively that in the larger scheme of things progress was inevitable. Even here, however, there were dark patches. Yet some evolutionists recognized a regressive potential in organisms, the so-called atavisms. Thus the Italian criminologist Cesare Lombroso lumped homosexuals together with criminals as throwbacks to a more primitive phase of human existence. Still humanity could maintain progress by blocking these atavisms and accelerate its course by eugenics.

The overall atmosphere of optimism and uplift notwithstanding, nineteenth-century realities led to a more somber view in some quarters. The countries of southern Europe were compelled to recognize that the pacesetters of material progress were found in northwestern Europe, and that they seemed to be falling inexorably further and further behind.

And here we find a major turning point.

It was in France that the theory of decadence emerged most fully and influentially. The word *décadence* had figured in the title of Montesquieu's *Considérations sur les causes de la grandeur des Romains et de leur décadence* (1747), and then of the French translation of Edward Gibbon's masterwork, and was thus redolent of the perennial problem of the reasons for Rome's decline. Gradually it came to indicate not simply a historical phase, but also a qualitative judgment on the state of civilization.

The word décadence was given a new twist by the French critic Desiré Nisard in 1834 as a pejorative term for certain literary trends of his own day. Nisard, whose professional interest was Latin literature, compared the mannerism and affectation of the Silver Age with certain aspects of the romanticism of his own day.

The defeat of France in the Franco-Prussian war (1870) induced an orgy of national self-examination, yielding in some quarters to a mood of resignation. In the 1880s the label decadence was actively embraced by the bisexual poet Paul Verlaine ("Langueur"), the novelist Joris-Karl Huysmans [A Rebours], and their followers. Joséphin Péladan, an advocate of androgyny, wrote a series of novels under the umbrella title La Décadence latine, implying that the whole of the Romance world was on the downward path. Others were fascinated by the regressive history of the Byzantine Empire and the perverse figure of Salome. While the "decadent" writers and artists soon found that it was more expedient to march under the banner of Symbolism, the association of their work with hot-house sophistication and rarified excess - in short the fin-de-siècle - had more staying power than the naysayers expected.

England, much influenced by nineteenth-century French cultural exports, had her own decadent writers and poets. The disgrace of the most notable of them, Oscar Wilde, in the three trials of 1895, sending repercussions throughout Europe, served for many to link the literary concept of decadence with the tactile immediacy (physical/visual images) of the perverted lifestyle.

In Germany Friedrich Nietzsche castigated the nineteenth century for its pervasive decadence, which he likened to the biological decline of an organism, but saw a possibility of renewal through the cultivation of Dionysiac art. Hitler was later to assert that homosexuality had destroyed ancient Greece - in which Sparta represented for National Socialism the ideal "Aryan civilization" - and that his Reich must avoid this fate.

As early as the 1920s leaders of Western Communist parties began to float the idea that the public discussion of homosexuality, and the seeming increase in homosexual activity, resulted from the decadence of capitalism, a system soon destined to disappear. In 1934 this approach resulted in new legal restrictions in the USSR. These measures were to remain in place throughout its existence, as seen in an article in the *Great Soviet Encyclopedia,* third edition of 1971. "Homosexuality (from gomo...and Lat. sexus–sex), a sexual perversion consisting in unnatural attraction to persons of the same sex. It occurs in persons of both sexes. The penal statutes of the USSR, the socialist countries and even some bourgeois states, provide for the punishment of homosexuality (muzhelozhestvo–sodomy between males)."

A recent variation on the decadence concept is the notion circulating in some quarters of African American opinion that sub-Saharan Africa was originally exempt from homosexuality, this perversion being forced on its inhabitants and their descendants in the New World as an instrument of colonial subjugation. In this perspective, homosexuality figures as part of the supposed pathology of the white race.

The ultimate origin of the meme of the sexual exceptionalism of Black Africa is probably Chapter XLIV of Edward Gibbon's *Decline and Fall of the Roman Empire* (1781): "I believe, and hope, that the negroes [sic], in their own country, were exempt from this moral pestilence." More recently, some observers from the Arab world have claimed, somewhat oddly, that there was no homosexuality in their lands before Western imperialists introduced it.

In any event, there is a growing body of evidence documenting homosexual behavior in Black Africa, both before and after colonization. Ironically it is the fear of homosexuality as a purported obstacle to progress and modernity that was forced on Africans by "enlightened" western opinion, not the practice itself.

In the United States anxiety about the prospect of national decline has been chronic ever since the 1950s. This concern has been lively, sometimes even alarmist. Yet a closer look shows that attention has focused chiefly on economic and political themes, not sexual ones.

In the 1950s, the Soviet space satellite Sputnik and the spread of Communism and Socialism through the postcolonial world were supposed proof of the economic efficiency and dedication to social justice characteristic of those systems and the rot of capitalism. By the 1970s and 1980s,

131

Japan Inc. emerged as the next new paradigm of the post-American world. As Japan faded, the next great hope followed in the 1990s, when the European Union seduced the American Left.

Yet something funny happened on this twisted path: Communism imploded; Japan is aging and shrinking; and the European Union is crumbling. But, of course, there is China, which, we are told, is the new replacement for America. Yet it is a country with serious demographic problems, a reputation for crude diplomacy, a muscular approach to international commercial agreements, censored media, vast inequality, environmental abuse, and a rigid political system seeking to manage the transition from a rural peasant society into postindustrial affluence.

Other explanations are more general. The historian Mancur Olson maintained that nations decline because their aging institutions become bloated and sclerotic, retarding national dynamism. The popular writer Charles Murray holds that America is coming apart, dividing into two nations - one with high levels of education, stable families, and good opportunities, vs. the other with low levels of education, unstable families, and poor opportunities.

Singly and in combination, all these issues pose a serious economic challenge to which the United States must respond. But the problem has no connection with a supposed decadence fostered by toleration of homosexuality. As LGBT individuals marry and build families the old explanation that they are simply selfish and unstable has become unviable. Moreover, as Richard Florida's studies of the creative class have shown, it is the most innovative sections of our nation, from Silicon Valley in California to the Boston region in Massachusetts, that are the most accepting of homosexuality. Sexual tolerance is not the problem, but part of the solution.

We conclude on a lighter note. The term "decadence" has been detoxified, as it were, by a New Orleans event that has become an institution. Southern Decadence is an annual six-day jamboree that occurs over Labor Day Weekend, climaxing with a parade through the French Quarter. The event traces its beginnings to a party of a group of 40 or 50 friends that was held in August 1972. They billed it the "Southern Decadence Party: Come As Your Favorite Southern Decadent."

"Decadence," as the observance is commonly dubbed by participants, is marked by street processions, bead tossing, and revelers promenading (often until the wee hours of the next morning) from one endless dance party to another. In these ways it resembles New Orleans' Mardi Gras. Yet Southern Decadence tends to be more sexual in tone and is generally geared towards more upscale and mature revelers. Decadence crowds in the Quarter remain true to their name, typically matching and sometimes exceeding Mardi Gras crowds.

Now That Is Decadent!

*Response.* Overall, the conventional wisdom goes something like this. The symptoms of social decadence are economic recession and dislocation; population decline; cor-

133

ruption; excessive luxury; widespread neurasthenia; social alienation and unrest; moral license; collapse of trust; and lack of honesty. Homosexuality often joins this list. Specifically, it has been claimed that the homosexual person, by withdrawing from the procreative pool, contributes to population decline. This is a demographic situation which now (for example, in Western Europe) provokes anxiety. Similar sentiments occurred in the old Soviet Union.

Let us try to penetrate somewhat further into the mindset that sustains such thinking.

Are the factors cited in the above indictment mere symptoms or actual causes? To the extent that homosexuality, say, is merely a sign of an underlying malaise, would it make sense to combat it? It might seem that anti-homosexual measures are the equivalent of arbitrarily slaying the messengers, merely for doing their job in bringing focus (of a sort) to the issues.

As these questions show, thinking about decadence tends to be complex and emotionally fraught, so that symptoms and causes are thrown together helter-skelter.

These varied aspects notwithstanding, the popular mind still seeks to blame homosexuality for the fate of Greece and Rome.

Can this charge be sustained? The expansive age of Greece from the seventh through the third century BCE was, according to our documentation, their age of idealized pederasty. Far from causing a decline in population, this flowering of same-sex love accompanied an almost explosive increase in population, requiring the foundation of colonies throughout much of the Mediterranean world and later the conquests of Alexander the Great in western Asia. Conversely, the period of Greek decline - the second and first centuries BCE - corresponded to an incipient sexual puritanism and a glorification of heterosexual married life.

As for Rome, most of the homosexual scandals reported by such writers as Suetonius and Tacitus belong to the great age of the first and second century; according to Gibbon the latter century ranks as one of the greatest ages of human happiness. Only in the fourth century, under the Christian emperors, did the Roman state take legal action against consensual male same-sex conduct. It was then that the Empire entered on its final downward glide, a process that had begun earlier.

In any event, the contemporary perspective is far different from the picture suggested by those old bogies.

Currently, the United States is facing a serious economic challenge. The gravity of this situation is undeniable. But the answer is better technology, not sexual repression. Today a billion adolescents worldwide are growing up with Apple iPhones, iPods, and iPads; with Facebook accounts, Twitter, Instant Text, Google searches; and with Amazon online ordering, and megastore discount purchasing. These are the reasons for America's strength and, as Richard Florida has shown, gay-friendly regions of the country tend to be more creative in these types of innovation than those that the regions that cling to traditional prejudices.

**BIBLIOGRAPHY**. J. Edward Chamberlain and Sander L. Gilman, eds., Degeneration: The Dark Side of Progress, New York: Columbia University Press, 1985; Louis Crompton, "What Do You Say to Someone Who Claims That Homosexuality Caused the Fall of Greece and Rome?" Christopher Street (March 1978), 49-52; Alexander Demandt, Der Fall Roms: Die Auflösung des Römischen Reiches im Urteil der Nachwelt, Munich: Beck, 1984; Paul Kennedy, The Rise and Fall of the Great Powers: Economic Change and Military Conflict From 1500 to 2000, New York: Random House, 1987; Andrew Sullivan, Virtually Normal: An Argument about Homosexuality, New York: Alfred A. Knopf, 1995; Richard L. Florida, The Rise of the Creative Class, and How It's Transforming Work, Leisure, Community and Everyday Life, New York: Basic Books, 2002.

# 4   *Homosexuals are irresistibly drawn to molest children (pedophilia).*

***The Charge.***   In 1999 the radio commentator Laura Schlessinger asserted that "a huge portion of the male homosexual populace is predatory on young boys." In fact, the boundaries between adult-adult homosexuality and pedophilia are fluid. In 2010 Tony Perkins of the Family Research Council noted: "While activists like to claim that pedophilia is a completely distinct orientation from homosexuality, evidence shows a disproportionate overlap between the two. ... It is a homosexual problem." For this reason homosexuals must never be allowed to serve in any profession that involves working with children or teenagers.

***Background.***   In recent decades concern with the sexual abuse of children and teenagers has spread in the United States and abroad. This anxiety has been heightened by widespread reports of abuse by Catholic priests and other religious figures, accompanied by the sense that the church authorities have been more committed to covering up the infraction than to punishing the abusers. These occurrences pose not only the physical problem (the sexual contact itself), but also the issue of psychological wrongness (the matter of misusing authority).

Understanding these issues is complicated by terminological confusion. Some observers use the term pedophilia to refer to all cases of sexual attraction to underage partners. Others restrict it to the preference for prepubertal children as sexual partners. Traditionally, sex with teenaged boys has been designated as pederasty. More recently, the term hebephilia has been proposed for adult attraction to adolescents.

Historians point to the fact that intergenerational sex has been common in such societies as ancient Greece, medieval Islam, and medieval Japan. However, these attitudes are not readily transferable to modern industrial societies in North America and Europe.

Empirical research in today's societies is hampered by the fact that most studies involve convicted perpetrators or pedophiles who have sought professional help. Clearly, these groups are subsets of a much larger population subject to such attractions. Some in this group never act on impulse and remain undetected. This is as it should be, as they have done nothing wrong. The available data suggests, however, that most pedophiles have never developed any sexual interest in adults, remaining fixated on children. For this reason they cannot be designated as merely homosexual.

The mistaken conflation of adult-adult homosexuality with adult-child behavior is being seen once more in 2013 in discussions concerning the current problems of the Catholic Church, which has been troubled for some time with reports of pedophile priests. Observers have noted the presence also of priests who have relations with other adult priests. These two groups are not the same.

*Response*. As the child-abuse specialist Nicholas Groth noted in 1982: "Homosexuality and homosexual pedophilia are not synonymous. In fact, it may be that these two orientations are mutually exclusive, the reason being that the homosexual male is sexually attracted to masculine qualities whereas the heterosexual male is sexually attracted to feminine characteristics, and the sexually immature child's qualities are more feminine than masculine.. . . . The child offender who is attracted to and engaged in adult sexual relationships is heterosexual. It appears, therefore, that the adult heterosexual male constitutes a greater sexual risk to underage children than does the adult homosexual male."

The mainstream view among researchers and professionals actively studying child sexual abuse is that homosexual men do not pose any special threat to children. Moreover, gay men and lesbians have a proven record of working effectively in a wide variety of employment settings. Research has revealed no significant differences between heterosexuals, bisexuals, and homosexuals in job performance. Nor is this true in terms of capacity to properly exercise authority in supervisory positions. Most importantly, the empirical research does not show that gay and bisexual men are any more likely than straight men to molest children.

One cannot argue that gay or bisexual men never molest children. It is of vital importance, however, to note that there is no scientific basis for claiming these men are more likely than heterosexual men to commit such an act. As has been noted, most child molesters cannot be characterized as having an adult sexual orientation. Their sexual-attraction patterns are directed exclusively to children.

*Note:* Some of the points indicated above derive from the

excellent posting by Professor Gregory Herek, University of California, Davis:

*http://psychology.ucdavis.edu/rainbow/html /facts_molestation.html.* See that source for further analysis and an extensive bibliography.

**BIBLIOGRAPHY**. A. Nicholas Groth and H. J. Birnbaum, "Adult Sexual Orientation and Attraction to Underage Persons," Archives of Sexual Behavior, 7:3 (1978), 175-181; A. Nicholas Groth and T. S. Gary, T. S. "Heterosexuality, Homosexuality, and Pedophilia: Sexual Offenses against Children and Adult Sexual Orientation," in A.M. Scacco, ed., Male Rape: A Casebook of Sexual Aggressions, New York: AMS Press. 1982, pp. 143-52; Theo Sandfort, Edward Brongersma, and A. X. van Naerssn, eds., Male Intergenerational Intimacy: Historical, Socio-psychological, and Legal Perspectives, New York: Haworth Press, 1991; E. O. Lauman, J. H. Gagnon, R. T. Michael, and S. Michaels, The Social Organization of Sexuality: Sexual Practices in the United States, Chicago: University of Chicago Press, 1994; Nathaniel McConaghy, "Paedophilia: A Review of the Evidence," Australian and New Zealand Journal of Psychiatry, 32:2 (1998), 252-65.

# 5 *Not indigenous in healthy countries, homosexuality is a form of corruption introduced from abroad.*

*The Charge.* This finding takes the following general form.

"The people of our sturdy nation would never have taken to homosexual vice on their own. Indeed our earliest records offer no indication of its occurrence. It was only when the corrupt [fill in blank], with their bad customs, came to our shores that some of our people succumbed to this temptation. Because of this intrusion, we have been troubled with this abomination ever since."

*Historical Background.* Such slurs represent a subset of the disdain some human groups show in ascribing the origin - or at least prevalence - of social failings to neighboring groups or peoples. Thus we speak of German measles, of taking French leave, and of going Dutch. In former times Italians blithely dubbed syphilis the mal francese (or morbus gallicus), while Frenchmen returned the compliment with their mal florentin (or mal de Naples).

Abraham Roback coined a useful term for this tendency towards name calling with reference to other nations. When a disparaging word or phrase that incorporates the name of a rival foreign city or country enters into that country's official lexicon - be it a phrase proper or even slang - it is called ethnophaulism.

In the case of homosexual behavior, ethnophaulism is not only a type of group slander, but it also reflects a curiosity to trace the custom to its purported source, in keeping with "popular diffusionism," which overlooks the possibility that such behavior patterns are human universals. Thus, in eighteenth-century England, where native homosexual behavior had been documented for centuries and when important innovations seem to have been occurring in the conceptualization of homosexual acts, the fashion continued to blame the custom on Italy.

Divided as they were into many competing city states, the Greeks were given to attributing unusual sexual predilections to their neighboring (albeit Hellenic) groups - as well as to foreigners.

Ostensibly special proficiency in fellatio obtained among the inhabitants of the island of Lesbos (its association with female homosexuality became commonplace only in comparatively recent times) and the alien Phoenicians. At various times unusual fondness for pederasty was remarked in Crete (Plato and others held that the institution began there), at Sparta, Chalcis, and on the island of Siphnos. Turning blatantly homosexual was sometimes called "taking ship for Messalia," after the ancient Greek colony on the site of modern Marseille, which perhaps acquired its renown through propinquity with the notoriously homosexual Celts. The Scythians, northern neighbors of the Greeks, were associated with a particular type of effeminacy. Among a basi-

142

cally tolerant people such as the Greeks, these ethnophaulic appellations have more the character of a bemused chiding than harsh reproof, much as we would say today "X is German and likes to work hard," or "Y's Scottish background makes him thrifty."

In the first century CE the Roman writer Cornelius Nepos seems to have been the first to describe pederasty simply as "Greek love." The Romans themselves were often charged with special devotion to the "posterior Venus" with various word plays on the palindrome Roma = Amor.

In later times in Europe there were various expressions associating sodomy with Italy. In 1422 the Zurich Rat- und Rechtbuch, a legal text, designated the practice by the verb florenzen, suggesting that the city of Florence had developed a particular reputation in this regard. Pierre de Brantôme (ca. 1540-1614) described the fashion for lesbian liaisons in sixteenth-century France with the Italian phrase "donna con donna" (lady with lady). At the courts of Louis XII and XIV male homosexual proclivities were traced to Italy, as in the Sun King's sarcastic comment "La France devenue italienne!" In England Sir Edward Coke (1552-1634) maintained that Lombard bankers had introduced sodomy in the late Middle Ages, while in the eighteenth century Italian opera was held to be a source of new infection. Ironically, Mussolini was later to reject a proposal to criminalize homosexuality in his country on the grounds that its practice was limited to rich foreign tourists.

The rural inhabitants of Albania, who until recently boasted an indigenous tradition of pederasty, nonetheless

143

sometimes designated their custom as madzupi, derived from madzup, "Gypsy," implying that pederasty had been brought in from the outside by this wandering people.

Some French writers localized the custom in other zones of the Mediterranean littoral. French trade with Arab countries and the occupation of North Africa (beginning in 1830) probably account for the popularity of such expressions as moeurs levantines and moeurs arabes. Just after the turn of the century, the Krupp and Eulenburg-von Moltke scandals contributed greatly to the popularity in a hostile France of the expression vice allemand, apparently reviving a notion current West of the Rhine in the time of Frederick II the Great - in the second half of the eighteenth century.

The temptation to hurl such charges becomes particularly great in wartime as seen in a shoddy pamphlet by Samuel Igra, Germany's National Vice (London, 1945), which even alleges that Hitler had been a male prostitute. A more general type of ethnophaulism, found in some Third World countries, claims that the Western industrial nations are declining because of their tolerance of "unnatural vice."

A recent variation of the meme is the notion circulating in some quarters of African American opinion that sub-Saharan Africa was originally untouched by homosexuality, this perversion being forced on its inhabitants and their descendants in the New World as part of the humiliation of colonialism. Ironically it is the fear of homosexuality as a purported obstacle to progress and modernity that was exported to Africa by "enlightened" western opinion, not the practice itself. The ultimate origin of the myth of the sexual exceptionalism of Black Africa is probably Chapter XLIV of Edward Gibbon's *Decline and Fall of the Roman Empire* (1781): "I believe, and hope, that the negroes [sic], in their own country, were exempt from this moral pestilence."

In April 2012 Uganda's president Yoweri Museveni remarked, "Before we came in touch with the Europeans, we had some few homosexuals. I want to inform the world that those homosexuals were not killed as some people are claiming... and they were not discriminated against. However, Africans are by nature discreet people. Even for heterosexuals."

*Response*. With increased study, all these claims have been found wanting. Not only is homosexuality, as Goethe observed, as old as the human race, it seems to be a cultural universal.

Edward Gibbon, who originated the myth of absence of homosexuality in Africa, had never been outside of Europe. Benefiting from better information, modern anthropology has reached quite different conclusions. Africa south of the Sahara presents a rich mosaic of peoples and cultures, and ongoing study is gradually completing the picture. For example, Stephen O. Murray has established that in a number of indigenous cultures, such as the Azande of the Sudan, the taking of boy-brides was a well-established custom. Among the Bantu-speaking Fang, homosexual intercourse was bian nku 'ma, a medicine for wealth, which was transmitted through anal penetration.

**BIBLIOGRAPHY**. Abraham Roback, A Dictionary

of International Slurs, Cambridge, MA: Sci-Art Publishers, 1944; Stephen O. Murray and Will Roscoe, Boy-wives and Female Husbands: Studies in African Homosexualities, New York: St. Martin's Press, 1998.

# 6  *As we know it, homosexuality is an innovation that appeared only a century and a half ago.*

*The Charge.* In keeping with the findings of Michel Foucault, historians of sexuality have established that homosexuality is a social invention that first arose in Europe as late as 1869. That is when the term "homosexual" was coined.

In all likelihood, same-sex acts, like other perversions, have always occurred in human history. But ours is the first society to have elevated this deplorable behavior to the status of a "lifestyle," complete with advocacy groups and university courses.

*Historical background.* The idea that the "modern homosexual" arose as late as 1869 is the thesis of a group of historians known as Social Constructionists. Their leader was the late Michel Foucault, who stressed the fact that the word "homosexual" was introduced in 1869. Referring to this presumed turning point Foucault famously remarked: "The sodomite had been a temporary aberration; the homosexual was now a species." ("Le sodomite était un relaps, l'homosexuel est maintenant une espèce." *Histoire de la sexualité*, vol. 1, Paris, 1976). Actually, the English-language version of the sentence does not fully capture the nuance of Foucault's wording, but it is this formula that has been influential.

In fact the first known appearance of the term homosexual in print occurs in an 1869 German pamphlet, *Paragraph 143 des Preussischen Strafgesetzbuchs und seine Aufrechterhaltung als 152 des Entwurfs eines Strafgesetzbuchs für den Norddeutschen Bund* ("Paragraph 143 of the Prussian Penal Code and Its Maintenance as Paragraph 152 of the Draft of a Penal Code for the North German Confederation") The pamphlet was created by the independent scholar Károly Mária Kertbeny, who wrote anonymously. The author advocated the repeal of Prussia's sodomy laws. Kertbeny had previously proposed the neologism in a private letter written in 1868 to Karl Heinrich Ulrichs. Kertbeny used Homosexualität in place of Ulrichs' Urningtum; Homosexualisten ("male homosexualists") instead of Urninge, and Homosexualistinnen ("female homosexualists") instead of Urninden. In succeeding years the new coinage spread into other languages, including English, prevailing for a long time as the standard term.

Together with Foucault, another major influence was the English sociologist Mary McIntosh. In 1968, she published a paper entitled "The Homosexual Role" in the journal *Social Problems*. Opposing the idea that homosexuality was a clinical pathology, she maintained that same-sex relations shifted in meaning and practice according to historical and cultural circumstances. There is no universally fixed homosexual, just shifting historical categories and linked experiences.

Though the Social Construction historians who followed in the wake of Foucault and McIntosh acknowledge that same-sex contacts occurred before 1869, they claim that they were merely acts, behavior that anyone could engage in. There was no distinct category, the "homosexual." To deny this point, the historians averred, was to commit the mistake of essentialism, disregarding the malleability of human behavior.

Along somewhat similar lines, Alfred Kinsey in his two famous *Reports* of 1948 and 1953 counseled against using "homosexual" and "heterosexual" as nouns. He held that they should only be employed as adjectives, characterizing conduct not status.

Until recently the main emphasis of the Social Construction scholars has been chronological, as seen in their effort to restrict the span of homosexuality to a mere 142 years. The corollary, its limitation to Western culture, was implicit but not stressed However, Joseph Massad, a professor of Palestinian origin at Columbia University, has taken up this cause, with special reference to the Arab world.

Massad's 2007 book *Desiring Arabs* offers a highly selective intellectual history of the Arab world and its Western representations in the nineteenth and twentieth centuries. Methodologically, Massad depends heavily on Edward Said's study of *Orientalism* of 1979, as well as on the work of Michel Foucault.

Massad maintains that "Western male white-dominated" gay activists, operating under the umbrella of what he terms the "Gay International," have undertaken a "missionary" effort to impose the heterosexual/homosexual dichotomy

149

onto cultures where no such binary mentality exists. In this way, he claims, these activists inflict on these cultures the very structures they challenge in their own home countries. Massad holds that "[t]he categories gay and lesbian are not universal at all and can only be universalized by the epistemic, ethical, and political violence unleashed on the rest of the world by the very international human rights advocates whose aim is to defend the very people their intervention is creating."

While the book was well received by specialists, some have noted an unfortunate effect on the international human-rights movement. For example, Rayyan Al-Shawaf, a free-lance writer living in Beirut, observes that "Massad's relativism - stemming from his accurate observation that 'homosexuality' is alien to Arab same-gender sexual traditions - is so extreme that he refuses to support a call for universal freedom of sexual identity." Writing in 2008 in the periodical Demokratiyya, Al-Shawaf argues that "in postulating the inevitability of (heterosexual) Arab violence wherever there is gay and lesbian assertiveness, Massad pre-emptively exonerates the perpetrators - whether individuals or the state - of any wrongdoing. However regrettable their behaviour, those Arabs who react violently to the gay rights campaign are not perceived by Massad as responsible for their actions, but as caught up in a broader struggle against 'imperialism,' to which the gay rights movement is wedded."

The upshot of Massad's condemnation of the "Gay International" is the admonition that Westerners must never attempt to interfere with restrictions on sexual variation anywhere in the non-Western world. Such interventions would amount to cultural imperialism.

Perhaps the most eloquent refutation of this view is found in a speech given by the US Secretary of State Hillary Clinton in Geneva on December 6, 2011.

She noted there is "a question of whether homosexuality arises from a particular part of the world. Some seem to believe it is a Western phenomenon, and therefore people outside the West have grounds to reject it. Well, in reality, gay people are born into and belong to every society in the world. They are all ages, all races, all faiths; they are doctors and teachers, farmers and bankers, soldiers and athletes; and whether we know it, or whether we acknowledge it, they are our family, our friends, and our neighbors.

"Being gay is not a Western invention; it is a human reality. And protecting the human rights of all people, gay or straight, is not something that only Western governments do. South Africa's constitution, written in the aftermath of Apartheid, protects the equality of all citizens, including gay people. In Colombia and Argentina, the rights of gays are also legally protected. In Nepal, the supreme court has ruled that equal rights apply to LGBT citizens. The Government of Mongolia has committed to pursue new legislation that will tackle anti-gay discrimination.

"Now, some worry that protecting the human rights of the LGBT community is a luxury that only wealthy nations can afford. But in fact, in all countries, there are costs to not protecting these rights, in both gay and straight lives lost to

151

disease and violence, and the silencing of voices and views that would strengthen communities, in ideas never pursued by entrepreneurs who happen to be gay. Costs are incurred whenever any group is treated as lesser or the other, whether they are women, racial, or religious minorities, or the LGBT. Former President Mogae of Botswana pointed out recently that for as long as LGBT people are kept in the shadows, there cannot be an effective public health program to tackle HIV and AIDS. Well, that holds true for other challenges as well."

*Response.* In its original form, the Social Construction argument rested on the fallacy that assumes that "where there is no term, there is no concept." Clearly this is to put the cart before the horse.

For example, international relations existed for many centuries before the introduction of the word "international" in the eighteenth century. Similarly, Karl Marx never used the term "capitalism" in his writings (though he did speak of capital). Still, it would be foolish to deny that the concept of capitalism is integral to Marx's thought. In instances such as these the concept and practice take hold before the label appears. Naming is secondary.

Behaviorally, the Social Construction claim of the invention of homosexuality in the second half of the nineteenth century simply does not hold up. We have abundant information on gay conduct from ancient Egypt, ancient Greece and Rome, medieval Islam, Renaissance Italy, and many other cultures. Historians such as Louis Crompton, Rictor Norton, William A. Percy, Michael Rocke - reputable scholars who reject the blinkered assumptions of the Social Constructionists - have abundantly documented this reality. In addition to his coverage of Europe, Crompton also deals with China and Japan, reinforcing the work of specialists in the history of those countries.

**BIBLIOGRAPHY**. Edward Stein, ed., Forms of Desire: Sexual Orientation and the Social Constructionist Controversy, New York; Routledge,1992; Rictor Norton, The Myth of the Modern Homosexual: Queer History and the Search of Identity, London: Cassell, 1997; Louis Crompton, Homosexuality and Civilization, Cambridge, MA: Belknap Press of Harvard University Press, 2003.

# 7   *The main cause of male homo-sexuality is fear of women.*

***The Charge.*** For a long time perceptive writers and social scientists have observed a tendency among men to fear women (gynecophobia).

To be sure, both heterosexual and homosexual men harbor this fear, a regrettable constant of Western civilization. The idea surfaced in classical and medieval thought. Later it entered into the revealing nineteenth-century obsession with the "femme fatale," or fatal woman, a seductress who delights in subjugating and controlling men.

For the most part heterosexual men are strong enough to overcome this anxiety - at least one would hope so. By contrast, men destined to become homosexual harbor the fear to an extraordinary degree. Hence male homosexuality reflects not so much an attraction to men, as a flight from women. If only these unfortunates could get help - from a counselor, life coach, therapist, or guru - they might be able to free themselves from their crippling disability. They would then find themselves able to lead productive lives as responsible husbands who cherish and honor women.

Instead, homosexuals resort to various evasions and coverups. They do this by cultivating friendships with token women. Sometimes a gay male will induce one to appear with him at very public social functions, where she must masquerade as his girlfriend. These unfortunate ac-

154

complices, known as "beards," disparage their gender as a whole. In much the same way the homosexual selects a particular woman to be his confidante - known as his "fag hag." In private, though, these poor accomplices are often pitied by the rest of society for lacking an identity, settling for a sham relationship that can never offer them sexual fulfillment.

Other women, more sensible, are alert to the insult that the exclusive preferences of gay men pose to them.

***Historical Background.*** The primordial image of the toxic, fearsome woman is the Medusa of ancient Greece. This monster had the face of a hideous human female sporting a tangle of venomous snakes in place of hair. Gazing directly upon her would turn onlookers to stone. Later, Freud was to regard the Medusa as an emblem of the male fear of castration.

Less sinister are the Greek images of the anasyrma, a rite of lifting the skirt in a defiant display of the female genitals. Medieval figures of the Sheela na Gig show a similar form of genital presentation. While scholars disagree about the exact meaning of these figures, they all convey a sense of the power of the female principle.

By contrast, the biblical figure of Eve was ambiguous. Even though she was the temptress responsible for the Fall, Eve was still the first mother of all mankind.

During the Middle Ages, the witchcraft delusion focused on unfortunate old women who were singled out and stigmatized for their supposed power to cast spells and cause other mischief.

In later times the femme fatale emerged as the modern archetype of the mysterious and seductive woman, whose charms ensnare her admirers in bonds of irresistible desire. Often she will lead them into compromising, dangerous, and even deadly situations.

In early versions of the theme, her ability to hypnotize her victim with a spell counts as literally supernatural. Even in later incarnations the femme fatale is commonly described as having power over men akin to that of an enchantress, seductress, vampire, witch, or demon.

The Marquis de Sade created several celebrated examples, including the heroine of his novel *Histoire de Juliette* (1797-1801), where the dangerous woman triumphs. During the Romantic period, the femme fatale continued to thrive, as seen in the works of the poet John Keats, notably "La Belle Dame sans Merci" and "Lamia."

In the late nineteenth and early twentieth centuries, the femme fatale became even more prominent: she flaunts her wiles in the lurid paintings of Edvard Munch, Gustav Klimt, Franz von Stuck, and Gustave Moreau; as well as in the canvases of the English pre-Raphaelite painters.

Oscar Wilde reinvented this archetype in his "Salome," a work that stands at the pinnacle of fin-de-siècle decadence, In this play (written in French in 1891), Salome mesmerizes her lust-crazed uncle King Herod with her enticing Dance of the Seven Veils. He has no choice but to yield to her imperious demand: "bring me the head of John the Baptist." Fittingly, Wilde's text was adorned with illustrations by the lubricious Aubrey Beardsley.

In his 1903 book *Sex and Character*, the Viennese writer Otto Weininger held that all people are a mixture of male and female elements. Purportedly, the male aspect rejoiced in the following positive attributes: it is active, productive, conscious, and moral/logical. By contrast, Weininger stigmatized the female aspect as passive, unproductive, unconscious, and amoral/alogical.

Weininger believed that emancipation was only possible for "masculine women" (aka butch lesbians). For most women, he held, the female life was dominated by the sexual function: either in the form of the act itself (amounting to prostitution) or in its more respectable guise (motherhood). Weininger - who committed suicide at the age of 23 - was probably a self-hating homosexual who loathed the feminine characteristics he detected in his own makeup. Once widely influential, Weininger's book is now seen as a period piece.

For their part, psychiatrists and social scientists have attempted to put the understanding of the fear of women on a more rational basis. A pioneer in this endeavor was Karen Horney, a German psychoanalyst and critic of Freudian theory. Somewhat tentatively, she stated her conclusions in her 1932 paper on "the dread of woman." Later, Erich Neumann, a German-born Jungian analyst, dedicated an essay to the subject entitled "The fear of the feminine" ("Die Angst vor dem Weiblichen," 1959). Neumann regarded "patriarchal normality as a form of fear of the feminine."

A contemporary contributor to the discussion is Chris Blazina, a psychodynamic psychologist and professor based at Tennessee State University. In 1997 Blazina asserted that "the fear of the feminine helps define what is masculine." In a paper of 1986 James O'Neil and his associates posited that the male fear of the feminine is a core aspect of the male psyche. They developed a 37-question psychometric test, a gender role conflict scale (GRCS), to measure the extent to which a man is in conflict with traditional masculine role values. This test relied upon the notion of the male fear of the feminine.

Werner Kierski, a London-based German-born psychotherapist and researcher, designed an empirical research program concerning the male fear of the feminine. Published in 2007, the results indicated that when men experience vulnerable feelings and/or other feelings associated with women, men can become frightened. According to Kierski, the fear of the feminine then acts in two ways: a) it takes the form of an internal monitor to ensure that men stay within the boundaries of what is regarded as masculine, i.e. being action-oriented, self-reliant, guarded, and seemingly independent; and b) if a man fails to achieve this status - thus feeling out of control, vulnerable, or dependent - the fear of the feminine can act as a defense, leading to splitting off, repressing, or projecting these feelings. Kierski concluded that male fear of the feminine can have a strong influence on both heterosexual and homosexual men.

Curiously, the research suggests that there appears to be a link between fear of the feminine and men's negative views towards counseling and psychotherapy. In other words, for whatever reason, patients aren't buying it. In addition, the research pointed to four possible groups of experiences that tend to foster male fear of the feminine: 1. experiencing vulnerability and uncertainty; 2. meeting women who are strong and competent; 3. confronting women who are angry and/or aggressive; 4. encountering women who are like their mothers.

The early years of the modern gay and lesbian liberation movement saw tension between men and women activists. Some lesbians held they were undervalued by gay men, who relegated them to subordinate positions. Yet by the beginning of the twenty-first century, as it had become clear that lesbian women and gay men working together had made great strides forward, much of this tension had abated.

In a way that would have appalled Otto Weininger a century ago, trans people are now widely accepted and even admired. They challenge all of us to ask fundamental questions about gender and our own place within its complex configuration.

Still, not everyone today agrees with this enlightened view. Some macho men continue to decry gay men as feminine; along with women, they are seen as objects of disdain and even violence. Recently, one young male blogger, Alex B., put it this way: "In all honesty, we hate the f*ck out of gay people because they act like women. Gay people are men that act like women. . . Totally uncool."

Much homophobic activity (including gay-bashing) stems from misogynistic beliefs that disparage traits mainstream society perceives as feminine. These are qualities that are embraced by some gay men. These traits include preoccupation with personal appearance, heightened emotionality, artistic flair, and lack of prowess in physically demanding activities - especially sports.

*Response*. In view of the genuine friendships that link heterosexual women and gay men, the blanket allegation of this fear is unwarranted, or at least greatly exaggerated, for its supposed workings do not constitute a barrier to social intimacy. Moreover, many gay men admire "strong women" because of their ability to challenge patriarchal norms that oppress them, for these same archaic notions serve to stifle LGBT people as well.

Some gay men are instinctually turned off by the female genitalia. That said, this negative response does not produce a positive attraction to their own sex. Arising from the most basic realm of the personality, this attraction responds to the perceived qualities of the male gender itself. By contrast, if aversion to women were the sole factor involved it would simply produce celibacy and asexuality. Attraction to members of one's own sex is a positive force, not a product of absence.

**BIBLIOGRAPHY**. Karen Horney, "The Dread of Woman: Observations on a Specific Difference in the Dread Felt by Men and by Women for the Opposite Sex," International Journal of Psycho-Analysis, 13 (1932), 348-60; Katharine M. Rogers, The Troublesome Helpmate: A History of Misogyny in Literature, Seattle: University of Washington Press, 1968; Bram Dijkstra, Idols of Perversity: Fantasies of Feminine Evil in Fin-De-Siecle Culture, New York: Oxford University Press, 1986; idem, Evil Sisters: The Threat of Female Sexuality in Twentieth-Century Culture, New York: Knopf, 1996; Jack Holland, Misogyny: The World's Oldest Prejudice, New York: Carroll and Graf, 2006; Werner Kierski and Christopher Blazina, "The Male Fear of the Feminine and Its Effects on Counseling and Psychotherapy," The Journal of Men's Studies, 17:2 (March 2009), 155-83.

# 8 Homosexuality is typically an aristocratic vice and is generally absent from the common person - unless suborned by money or favors.

*The Charge*. Over the centuries, indulgence in homosexual behavior has been more prevalent among wealthy, privileged people than among ordinary folk. There are two main schools of thought on this phenomenon. The predilection could be a) hereditary and constitutional; or b) cultural and environmental.

The hereditary approach claims that through inbreeding the aristocratic stock has become effete and degenerate. This factor has been explored by such perceptive writers as Joris-Karl Huysmans, Max Nordau, and Marcel Proust.

The other approach, emphasizing culture and environment, notes that the wealthy and privileged tend to pamper themselves with all sorts of indulgences including fancy meals, liqueurs, and prostitutes of either the opposite or the same sex. In order to satisfy their blood lusts and other proclivities, they prey on the working class. Feigning unawareness of the consequences of their behavior, they turn a blind eye to conscience or regret. Their soulless aim is to use their money and privilege to corrupt innocent youth. This deplorable pattern was ornately illustrated by the careers of Lord Alfred Douglas and his partner in crime, the playwright, poet, and epigramist Oscar Wilde.

Education (classical studies and travel in particular) acquaints privileged classes with "variant" forms of sexual behavior. This background encourages them in their folly that they can yield to this indulgence with impunity. In addition, the confinement of young men in one-sex schools, as in England, has tended to encourage such deviance.

***Historical Background.*** In reality, little meaningful study has been accomplished on the role that class differences play in the incidence of same-sex behavior. The findings of the first Kinsey *Report* (1948), which appeared to show greater prevalence of homosexuality among the less educated, have been criticized, because of the large proportion of prisoners included, individuals who tend to be poor and disadvantaged.

In the absence of concrete data, stereotypes have flourished.

The notion of homosexuality as a distinctively aristocratic vice has a considerable history. In the seventeenth century Sir Edward Coke attributed the origin of sodomy to "pride, excess of diet, idleness and contempt of the poor." The noted English jurist was in fact offering a variation on a formula found in the prophet Ezekiel (16:49). This accusation reflects the perennial truism that wealth, idleness, and lust tend to go together - a cluster summed up in the Latin term luxuria. Sometimes the view is expressed that the confirmed debauchee, having run through virtually the whole gamut of sexual sins, turns to sodomy as a last resort

163

to revive a jaded appetite.

A forerunner of this thought complex appears in the ancient Greek comedies of Aristophanes (ca. 450-385 BCE), who satirized the pederastic foibles of Athenian politicians and dandies. In the first century of our era, the Jewish writer Philo of Alexandria regarded Sodom as the archetype of the link between homosexuality and luxury: "The inhabitants owed this extreme license to the never-failing lavishness of their sources of wealth. . . . Incapable of bearing such satiety, plunging like cattle, they threw off from their necks the law of nature, applied themselves to deep drinking of strong liquor... dainty feeding and forbidden forms of intercourse."

The scholastic theologian Albertus Magnus (d. 1280) held that the vice of sodomy was "more common in persons of high station than in humble persons." This impression reflects in part the greater visibility of the doings of the privileged, and also the fact that, through their status or influence, the nobility could frequently escape with a reprimand for the commission of crimes which were subject to capital punishment when committed by commoners. This aspect of class justice has fueled social envy, leading to the demand on the part of the straitlaced middle class that the aristocracy be disciplined and compelled to adhere to the narrow canons of petty bourgeois morality.

In England the claim that homosexuality was an aristocratic failing fell together with the prejudice that the predilection for the behavior was of foreign derivation; the fondness of the noble lords for the Grand Tour of the continent brought them into contact with the vice - which they then conveyed to England, where it was supposedly not native. A curious episode of this phase of British social history was the Macaroni Club, an association of cosmopolites formed in London about 1760 to banquet on that exotic cuisine. Their foppish, extravagant dress was regarded as bordering on transvestism. This fashion explains an otherwise mysterious allusion in an American song of the period: "Yankee Doodle came to town/upon a little pony;/ he stuck a feather in his hat/and called it macaroni" (1767). The colonial dandy's attempt to play the exquisite exposed him to the danger of ridicule as a milquetoast - or worse.

The stereotype of aristocratic vice has a sequel in the early twentieth-century Marxist notion that the purported increase of homosexuality in modem industrial states stems from the decadence of capitalism; in this view the workers fortunately remain psychologically healthy and thus untainted by the debilitating proclivity. In the Krupp and von Moltke-Eulenburg scandals in Germany in 1903-08, journalists of the socialist press did their best to inflame their readership against the unnatural vices of the aristocracy, which were bringing the nation to the brink of ruin.

In the late nineteenth century, homosexual vanguard writers such as Edward Carpenter and John Addington Symonds maintained an opposing thesis. They held that it was precisely the fact that gay contacts tended to link the rich and the poor, the educated and the uneducated, that made them suited to advancing democracy and the social integration of previously antagonistic classes.

165

While gay men like Carpenter and Symonds have idolized the working class, others do just the opposite. These people are fascinated by the doings of members of the British and European nobility, especially the royals. A recent instance of this penchant was the massive outpouring of grief among gay men over the death of Diana, Princess of Wales, who died in a car accident in Paris on August 31, 1997.

*Response*. Class differences persist in these our modern times. Yet film and television, together with popular music, are helping to promote a common culture. Coeducational schools are now the norm. With the fading of overt class markers, the problem of the "aristocratic vice" seems merely historical,

**BIBLIOGRAPHY**. Matt Cook, ed., A Gay History of Britain: Love and Sex Between Men since the Middle Ages, Oxford: Greenwood, 2007.

# 9 *Clannish and secretive, gays are prone to banding together against the common good.*

*The Charge.* Clannishness among homosexuals is habitual. In many walks of life the Lavender Mafia is active, to the detriment of the general interests of society.

Such obnoxious preening instinctively forms its own circles in the workplace. And of course this behavior is blatant in the "gay" hell-holes that dare to promote themselves as legitimate entertainment. Not infrequently deviant sex occurs on the premises.

In daily life these reprobates commonly choose to live in "gay villages" - ghettos in effect - almost always located in the the most disreputable, run-down areas of our major cities.

Today, the Internet facilitates their deviant togetherness. Their affinity for self-segregating makes them a subversive element in society, one that must be ruthlessly exposed for what it is.

*Historical Background.* That this collectivist tendency has occurred to such an extent is a product of society's disparagement and persecution of homosexuals. Western society's historic effort to taboo deviant sexual expression has forced those with such orientations to adopt coded and clandestine means of communication. Thus in the nine-

167

teenth century the French critic Charles Auguste Sainte-Beuve (1804-1869) wrote of a freemasonry of love. In twentieth-century America the slang term mason (borrowed from hobo slang) has enjoyed some currency with the meaning "homosexual." In the late 1940s the organizational proposals of the pioneering gay activist Harry Hay led to the formation of the Mattachine Society. These arrangements were based on both the Freemasons and the Communist Party (in which Hay had been active). The term Mattachine served to disguise the aim of the group to outsiders, a tactic which struck some as devious, however necessary it may have been in that repressive era.

To homophobes the very existence of gay organizations, even with transparent names, seems conspiratorial by definition. For this reason, these haters speak of a gay agenda, as if there were some central body in which gays and lesbians gather clandestinely to draw up a list of desiderata, and then devise nefarious schemes to achieve them.

This notion, redolent of the appalling anti-Jewish fraud known as the *Protocols of the Elders of Zion*, had a precursor in the 1950s phantom of a Homintern or secret international society, which reputedly controlled culture and the arts. Apparently the term Homintern was coined by the poet W. H. Auden. The reference is to the Comintern, a coordinating agency created by Joseph Stalin to promote world Communism. Sometimes journalists used the expression Lavender Mafia to similar effect.

In point of fact the various international homosexual organizations have been too loosely organized to fulfill any such subversive function. The belief in a great homosexual conspiracy probably reflects a guilt formation on the part of some heterosexuals, who unconsciously fear that their bigotry merits such a response.

In a more informal sense gay cliques have developed in offices and other organizational settings. Initially, the members recognize one another by using their gaydar. Some of these cliques were indeed clandestine, meeting a minimalist definition of conspiracy. Today, with more integration of gay and straight people, this separatism is less significant.

Recently, the term Lavender Mafia has been used to designate a faction within the leadership and clergy of the Catholic Church that allegedly protects and advocates for the acceptance of homosexuality. Proponents of the theory decry "a heterosexual exodus from the priesthood," claiming that change this reflects the prevalence of blatant gay subcultures in many seminaries. This atmosphere discourages potential heterosexual seminarians from joining the priesthood. Early in 2013 it was rumored that the Lavender Mafia played a role in the resignation of pope Benedict XVI. Ostensibly, this cabal involves senior cardinals and other Vatican officials. who avidly participate in gay bars, saunas, chat rooms, while using male-prostitution services.

*Response*. Since their influence is often exaggerated and sensationalized, these associations or circles scarcely bear the awful weight of subversion that has been assigned to them. GLBT people are not that dangerous - even though some jokingly say that they wish they could be.

169

For their part, the more visible gay and lesbian out-fits are no different from the bonding of members of ethnic groups or fans of particular sports teams. Nowadays, the circles tend to be supplemented or replaced by gay caucuses - among journalists, college teachers, and businesspeople, to name a few groups. These groups operate openly, often with the encouragement of the employer. As such, they cannot be termed conspiracies. Increasingly, political life recognizes that gay men and lesbians have legitimate group interests, and that those with these concerns must be permitted to operate openly if they are to be properly pursued.

In recent years politicians have generally abandoned their wonted attitudes of scorn and indifference. Recognizing that GLBT people vote, politicians increasingly seek their support.

**BIBLIOGRAPHY**. Michael S. Sherry, Gay Artists in Modern American Culture: An Imagined Conspiracy, Chapel Hill: University of North Carolina Press, 2007; Frances Green, ed., Gayellow Pages, New York: Renaissance House, 2010.

## 10 *The US gay-rights movement is a manifestation of far-left subversion, and its goal is to destroy America as we know it.*

*The Charge.* How far we have traveled from the wisdom of earlier days! We all should honor the memory of a courageous speech by Senator Joseph R. McCarthy of Wisconsin at a Lincoln's Birthday dinner of a Republican League in Wheeling, West Virginia, on February 9, 1950. In his remarks McCarthy accused the Truman Administration of harboring "loyalty and security risks" in government service. And the security risks, he later told Congressional investigators, were in no small part made up of "sex perverts." A subcommittee of the Senate was duly formed to investigate his charges, with all seven members of the subcommittee endorsing them, and calling for more stringent measures to ferret out homosexuals in government.

Of course some naysayers scoffed. In fact, however, the modern gay rights movement was started by a group of card-carrying Communists in Los Angeles in the 1950s. As such, it was a plot devised in Moscow with the intent of weakening America's moral fabric. Alas, even though the Soviet Union is no more, the scheme succeeded all too well. In keeping with its far-left origins, the gay movement has remained antithetical to American values, seeking to forge a "new, progressive society," one in which no decent citizen would want to live.

***Historical Background.*** The ideas of Marx and Engels emerged from the ferment of radical thought that bubbled forth in Restoration Europe, an era that began in 1815. This ferment included positivist, empiricist, anarchist, socialist, and Christian-socialist strains.

Unlike the individualist utopian Charles Fourier, Marx and Engels showed little interest in sex and sexual orientation; indeed they were typical Victorians in this respect. There can be little doubt that, as far as they thought of the matter at all, Marx and Engels were personally homophobic, as shown by an acerbic 1869 exchange of letters on Jean-Baptiste von Schweitzer, a German socialist rival. Schweitzer had been arrested in a park on a morals charge and not only did Marx and Engels refuse to join a committee defending him, they resorted to the cheapest form of bathroom humor in their private comments about the affair. Similar lack of subtlety characterizes their views on the pioneering homophile theories of Karl Heinrich Ulrichs, in which they confused uranism with pederasty and pederasty with pedication (anal intercourse).

The only important sexual passage, however, in the body of work published in the lifetimes of the two founders occurs in Engels' *Origin of the Family, Private Property and the State* (1884): "Greek women found plenty of opportunity for deceiving their husbands. The men ... amused themselves with hetaerae, but this degradation of women was avenged on the men and degraded them till they fell into

172

the abominable practice of pederasty (Knabenliebe) and degraded alike their gods and themselves with the myth of Ganymede." Engels' tracing of the problem to heterosexual infidelities is curious in view of his own record of amorous adventurism.

As in Freudian psychoanalysis, the very question of what is orthodox in Marxism has incited an enormous debate. Marx himself ejected Mikhail Bakunin and other anarchists, all of whom by doctrine tolerated homosexuality, from the First International. Yet one is on firm ground in saying that Social Democracy (which also had non-Marxist roots) departed in two fundamental respects: it favored gradual reform instead of revolutionary upheaval; and held that attitudes could be changed before the economy was transformed - thus eroding the basic Marxist doctrine of the dependency of the cultural superstructure on the economic base.

In the 1890s, some Social Democrats like August Bebel and Eduard Bernstein in Germany sought to foster a more enlightened social attitude, advocating women's rights and the elimination of laws criminalizing homosexuals. Such efforts were largely conducted among intellectuals and bureaucrats who intuited that the masses were not yet prepared to discard inherited prejudices.

A few gay leftists have projected a rosy picture of homosexual life in Russia in the years after the 1917 revolution. Yet the abrogation of the tsarist law against sodomy was simply part of an overall rejection of the laws of the old regime and significantly, the Soviets never undertook any campaign to combat popular prejudice against homosexual-

173

ity, as they did, for example, against the misogyny, Great Russian chauvinism, and anti-Semitism. Also, despite much searching, no unequivocal statement in support of homosexual rights has ever been unearthed from the prolific writings of Lenin or Trotsky, even though both had lived in Western Europe at the time of the early German homosexual rights movement. Under Lenin Russian homosexuals fared no better - if even as well - as they had done in the last decades of tsarist rule, when such brilliant figures as Tchaikovsky, Kuzmin, and Kluev came to the fore.

In the 1920s some German homosexual movement figures such as Magnus Hirschfeld and Richard Linsert (the latter a minor Communist Party functionary in Berlin) were favorably impressed by reports suggesting enlightened attitudes in the Soviet Union - about which they had no direct knowledge. They appear to have been the victims of an early disinformation campaign on the part of the Soviets.

Not everyone was taken in. Although André Gide proclaimed his sympathy for the Soviet Union in 1932, four years later after visiting the country he wrote openly of his disillusionment. Aware of anti-homosexual legislation passed in 1934, he attempted to bring up the matter with Stalin, without success. On publishing his defection from the "Popular Front" line, Gide was attacked by French and Czechoslovak party stalwarts (who had previously lauded him to the skies) as a "poor bugger" who had mixed up "revolution and pederasty."

As early as the 1920s leaders of Western Communist parties began to float the idea that the public discussion of

174

homosexuality, and a seeming increase in homosexual activity, resulted from the decadence of capitalism in its death throes. Homosexuality was to disappear in the healthy new society of the future.

After the Nazis came to power in Germany in 1933, Marxist proponents of the decadence theory added a new layer to these attacks in their myth of "fascist perversion," some purported affinity between homosexuality and Nazism. Leftist propaganda of this type may have played a part in Hitler's decision to liquidate his homosexual henchman Ernst Röhm, thereby distancing himself from the accusation.

In June 1934 the exiled Marxian psychoanalyst Wilhelm Reich opined: "The more clearly developed the natural heterosexual inclinations of the juvenile are, the more open he will be to revolutionary idea; the stronger the homosexual tendency within him... the more easily he will be drawn to the right." More generally, the heterosexualism that is so salient in the Marxist tradition may have been augmented by the perceived link between production and reproduction. Most Marxists are, of course, heterosexual and, in keeping with the tendency of true-believer groups to exalt all their shared traits, subject to unthinking bias.

The fall of Communism in Eastern Europe and Russia in 1989-91 made that political movement obsolete, except for fossils like Cuba and North Korea. Following previous practice, the Communist parties that struggled to survive were generally unsympathetic to homosexual participation in their activities and indifferent to gay issues. In most western countries it has been Trotskyists, with their claustrophobic and faction-ridden experience of marginality, who have provided the few organizational havens open to gay people in the world Communist movement, such as it is nowadays.

Despite all this negativity, the contribution of Marxism to the movement for gay rights and to the interpretation of homosexual behavior itself merits separate consideration. When the second gay rights movement emerged in the form of the Mattachine Society in Los Angeles in 1950, a number of its leaders, preeminently Henry Hay, had backgrounds in the Communist Party (CP) of the United States. Hay used the CP model for the cellular structure he designed for Mattachine. In an era in which homosexuality was illegal in every American state, the organizational structure of a political group that had, in many countries, been forced into clandestinity in order to survive seemed relevant. The American Communist Party had also been in the forefront of the early struggle against racial segregation, and this example also proved attractive: gay rights as a form of civil rights.

When the US civil rights movement entered its major phase in the 1960s, Marxist groups continued active but were less prominent. At this time, however, they made a significant contribution to the organizing of the protests against the Vietnam war, though this was also permeated by New Left, anarchist, and hippie elements. This amalgam made its effect felt on the new gay organizations that arose in the wake of the Stonewall Rebellion of 1969 - especially the Gay Liberation Fronts of New York and other cities. At the same time Marxist influences had begun to permeate some sectors of renascent feminism; this channel contributed such organizational devices as consciousness raising and "political correctness."

There were also important international effects. Reflecting a number of events - such as the May 1968 insurrection in France, the anti-Vietnam War movement, unrest in the universities, and of course the Stonewall Rebellion of 1969 - militant gay liberation organizations sprang up around the world. Many saw their roots as lying more in left radicalism than in the established homophile groups of the time, such as the British Gay Liberation Group (which took its name from its short-lived American counterpart), the British Gay Left Collective, the Italian Fuori!, the French FHAR, the German Rotzschwule, and the Dutch Red Faggots. All these groups are now defunct.

A number of writers and leaders of this phase of the world gay-liberation movement came from a left-wing background, including David Fernbach (Britain), Daniel Guérin and Guy Hocquenghem (France), Mario Mieli (Italy), and Dennis Altman (Australia). Some of these figures took their cue from Herbert Marcuse's *Eros and Civilization*, a book that sought to combine the ideas of Karl Marx with those of Sigmund Freud.

The attitudes of some minor Marxist parties in the United States must be briefly noted. The Revolutionary Communist Party's policy that "struggle will be waged to eliminate [homosexuality] and reform homosexuals" wasn't abandoned until 2001. The RCP now supports gay liberation. Meanwhile, the more influential American Socialist Worker's Party (SWP) released a memo stating that gay oppression had less "social weight" than black and women's struggles, forbidding members from being involved in gay political organizations. They maintained that too close an association with gay liberation would give the SWP an "exotic image" and alienate it from the masses.

As the GLBT movement began to gain ground, Socialist organizations' policies evolved, and some groups actively campaigned for gay rights whether opportunistically or out of conviction. Examples of this positive approach are the feminist Freedom Socialist Party, the Party for Socialism and Liberation, the International Socialist Organization, and the Socialist Party USA. The last group ranks the first American political party to select an openly gay man for president, nominating David McReynolds in 1980.

These groups remained tiny. Even though McReynolds campaigned energetically for president, he only received 6,994 votes (0.01%) nationally in 1980.

By the late seventies the Marxist influence on the US gay liberation movement had peaked and was receding, a decline reflecting the perennial marginality of he revolutionary left in American political life. The arcane, even scholastic tone that suffused the intellectual discussions did not help.

Moreover, the imposition of Soviet-style totalitarianism in Castro's Cuba, formerly the idol of gay radicals, dashed many hopes, and rival visions came forward: anarchist, libertarian, and communitarian.

By the early years of the twenty-first century, veterans of the gay left had come to feel increasingly marginalized. The most important issue before the community was gay marriage - a mainstream, not a revolutionary issue. This cause was widely decried in surviving gay-left circles as one of the chief culprits in the trend towards "assimilationism," which they opposed. The ongoing commercialization of gay culture and everyday life also alienated the gay leftists, but they were powerless to oppose it.

*Response*. As the above review has shown, the various Communist parties, the cutting edge of the revolutionary left, have not proven reliable supporters of the cause of gay rights. It is true that Harry Hay and his colleagues, founders of Mattachine in 1950, were - most of them - Communists. In previous years Hay had been particularly zealous in honoring his CP commitment. Yet when his comrades learned of his initiative, Hay was forced to leave the Party. In those days Communists were just as homophobic as most of the rest of American society.

The Mattachine Society abandoned any connection with the far left in 1953, three years after the founding of the group. As it evolved, the GLBT movement has become more and more diverse. Nonetheless, its center of gravity today lies in groups that are allied with the Democratic Party. In affirming this connection, though, GLBT people are no different from African Americans. There are, however, two gay groups allied with the Republican Party: the Log Cabin Club and GOProud.

**BIBLIOGRAPHY**. Mario Mieli, Homosexuality and

Liberation: Elements of a Gay Critique. David Fernbach, trans. London: Gay Men's Press, 1980; John D'Emilio, Sexual Politics, Sexual Communities: The Making of a Homosexual Minority in the United States, 1940-1970, Chicago: University of Chicago Press, 1983; Hubert Kennedy, Gert Hekma, Harry Oosterhuis, and James D. Steakley, eds., Gay Men and the Sexual History of the Political Left, New York: Harrington Park Press, 1995; Sherry Wolf, Sexuality and Socialism: History, Politics, and Theory of LGBT Liberation, Chicago: Haymarket, 2009.

# 11  *Unable to reproduce, homosexuals must recruit to continue their group.*

*The Charge.* The allegation of recruitment was forcefully sustained by Anita Bryant in her heroic 1977 campaign to repeal a noxious ordinance in Miami-Dade County that banned discrimination on the basis of sexual orientation. Unfortunately, her insights have been somewhat neglected in recent years.

Central to Bryant's effort was her exposure of the role of homosexual recruitment. Bryant said "[a]s a mother, I know that homosexuals cannot biologically reproduce children; therefore, they must recruit our children." This imperative stems from the inability of same-sex couples to reproduce offspring.

Subsequently, these fundamental points were reinforced by Judith Reisman, together with some religious groups. Ins 1994 Reisman asserted that homosexual "recruitment is loud; it is clear; it is everywhere." She estimated the gay and lesbian population at the time to be 1-2% but predicted at least 20% (and possibly over 30%) "of the young population will be moving into homosexual activity" as a result of "recruitment" The concept of recruitment also underlies pedophilia, in which young boys are first groomed, then violated and turned into homosexuals.

*Background.* The idea is akin to the notion of religious

181

proselytizing, as seen in the contemporary phenomenon of Mormon and other missionaries going from door to door in search of converts. Although sodomy was sometimes compared with heresy in the middle ages, there is no evidence of sodomites proselytizing then or after.

Sex education programs have taken some flack for this. However, there is no evidence that they attempt to steer young people towards an embrace of the "homosexual lifestyle." If anything, these educational efforts tend to assume that heterosexuality is the norm. Some traditionalists oppose anti-bullying campaigns on the grounds that they coddle sissies - sometimes a codeword for fairies.

These concerns have not been limited to the United States. In the United Kingdom, Section 28 of the Local Government Act (1988) generated significant public controversy relating to the public presentation of homosexuality. This provision stipulated that a local authority "shall not intentionally promote homosexuality or publish material with the intention of promoting homosexuality" or "promote the teaching in any maintained school of the acceptability of homosexuality as a pretended family relationship." No prosecution was ever brought under this legislation, and following intense debate the section was repealed in 2003. Yet its enactment caused some schools in the UK to limit or self-censor, suppressing discussion (or "promotion") of homosexual and bisexual relationships (and by extension transgender and sexual-diversity issues as well) within classes, sex education, and student activities - for fear of breaching the law.

While the situation in Britain has changed, Russia is seeing indications of a similar tendency to prohibition of "homosexual promotion" (as of 2013).

Arguably, the allegation of homosexual recruitment finds a scintilla of truth in Harry Hay's launch of the Mattachine Society in Los Angeles in 1950. Basing himself on his experience in the political campaign in favor of Henry Wallace, Hay did energetically seek members for his new group. Yet the purpose of this and other GLBT tights organizations was never to form a "sex club" - far from it - but to work constructively together in order to improve the lives of all gay people.

*Response.* The demographic argument fails because gay men and lesbians can and do have children. Moreover, most young people who develop a homosexual orientation do so in a heterosexual household. Most report that their journey began with a lonely, gradually dawning understanding that they were irreversibly attracted to their own sex. If any recruiting took place, they recruited themselves. The gay orientation set in despite the intense heterosexual conditioning that surrounded them. Only after their own authentic being had become unmistakably clear to them, did these individuals begin to seek out peers who shared their sensibility.

**BIBLIOGRAPHY**. John D'Emilio, Sexual Politics, Sexual Communities: The Making of a Homosexual Minority in the United States, 1940-1970, Chicago: University of Chicago Press, 1983, John Loughery, The Other Side of Silence: Men's Lives and Gay Identities: A Twentieth-

Century History, New York: Henry Holt, 1998.

## 12 In defiance of the common good, gays pursue a homosexual agenda and demand special rights.

*The Charge.* Conservative Christians in the United States have correctly detected a "homosexual agenda" (or "gay agenda"), which zealously promotes cultural acceptance of abnormal relationships. These interventions are the mission of the so-called "gay-rights" organizations. They seek legal changes so as to provide special privileges for their group, as seen in anti-discrimination laws and gay marriage.

Despite their unconvincing denials, these groups are involved in recruiting heterosexuals for their nefarious purposes. They seek either to convert them outright to the "homosexual lifestyle" or to make them what they term "gay friendly." Some of the victims of this propaganda adopt the characteristic homosexual obsession with grooming and appearance; these individuals are known as "metrosexuals." This process contributes to the growing pansification of our society.

In a more sinister way those who pursue the gay agenda are seeking to normalize pedophilia, a criminal activity with abundant homosexual connections.

*Background.* This bugaboo is relatively recent. In the US, the term "the gay agenda" entered public discourse in 1992 when the Family Research Council, a conservative Christian group, released a video series called The Gay

Agenda as part of a pack of materials focusing on the "hidden gay agenda." In the same year the Oregon Citizens Alliance adopted this video as part of their campaign for Ballot Measure 9 to amend the Oregon Constitution to prevent what the OCA called special rights for gays, lesbians, and bisexuals. Paul Cameron, co-founder of the Institute for the Scientific Investigation of Sexuality in Lincoln, later renamed the Family Research Institute appeared in the video, asserting that 75 percent of gay men regularly ingest feces and that 70-78 percent have had a sexually transmitted disease. The first Gay Agenda video was followed by three other video presentations; The Gay Agenda in Public Education (1993), The Gay Agenda: March on Washington (1993), and a feature follow-up Stonewall: 25 Years of Deception (1994).

The label attaches to efforts to change government policies and laws on GLBT issues - such as same-sex marriage and civil unions, GBLT adoption, recognizing sexual orientation ad a protected civil-rights minority classification, GLTBT military participation, inclusion of GLBT history and themes in public education, introduction of anti-bullying legislation to protect minors - as well as nongovernmental campaigns and individual actions designed to increase visibility and cultural acceptance of GLBT people, relationships, and identities. The label has also been used by some social conservatives to characterize alleged goals of LGBT-rights activists, such a the purported recruiting of heterosexuals into what they term a "homosexual lifestyle."

Some Christian critics of GLGT rights also deploy the idea of a homosexual agenda to assail a putative ideology they refer to as homosexualism, using the term homosexualists to describe people who seek to advance GLBT emancipation. The use of homosexualist in this way figured in 1995 in Scott Lively and Kevin Abrams' 1995 book *The Pink Swastika*, where it was taken "to refer to any person, homosexual or not, who actively promotes homosexuality as morally and socially equivalent to heterosexuality as a basis for social policy."

According to a Christian Broadcasting Network article by Paul Strand, the book *After the Ball* stemmed from "a 1988 summit of gay leaders in Warrenton, Virginia, who came together to agree on the agenda" and that "the two men [Kirk and Madsen] proposed using tactics on 'straight' America that are remarkably similar to the brainwashing methods of Mao Tse-Tung's Communist Chinese - mixed with Madison Avenue's most persuasive selling techniques." The article goes on to claim that films such as *Brokeback Mountain* are part of this "well-planned propaganda campaign."

In 2003 US Supreme Court Justice Antonin Scalia wrote in his dissent in the landmark case Lawrence v. Texas that "[t]oday's opinion is the product of a Court, which is the product of a law-profession culture, that has largely signed on to the so-called homosexual agenda, by which I mean the agenda promoted by some homosexual activists directed at eliminating the moral opprobrium that has traditionally attached to homosexual conduct."

In 2005 James Dobson, director of Focus on the Family, described the homosexual agenda as follows: "Those goals include universal acceptance of the gay lifestyle, discrediting of scriptures that condemn homosexuality, muzzling of the clergy and Christian media, granting of special privileges and rights in the law, overturning laws prohibiting pedophilia, indoctrinating children and future generations through public education, and securing all the legal benefits of marriage for any two or more people who claim to have homosexual tendencies."

*Response.* The Gay and Lesbian Alliance against Defamation (GLAAD) characterizes the expression homosexual agenda as a "rhetorical invention of anti-gay extremists seeking to create a climate of fear by portraying the pursuit of civil rights for LGBT people as sinister." Campaigns based on a presumed "gay agenda" have been described as anti-gay propaganda by researchers and critics. GLAAD describes the linkage of homosexuality with pedophilia or child molestation as an attempt to "insinuate that lesbians and gay men pose a threat to society, to families, and to children in particular." GLAAD considers assertions linking pedophilia and homosexuality to be defamatory, damaging, and entirely inaccurate.

The most telling objection to the disparaging allegation of a gay agenda is this. Under American democracy all groups are permitted to organize in order to achieve their basic rights. In this light, most gay spokespeople agree on certain goals, including rejection of the sodomy laws and other harmful legislation, as well as same-sex marriage. Advocating these goals does not constitute any demand for "special rights," but simply a petition for equality of treatment. Moreover, since all sorts of other groups - including those favoring protection of the environment and opposing cruelty to animals - organize to advance their goals, why should GLBT people be barred from doing so?

**BIBLIOGRAPHY**. Marshall Kirk and Hunter Madsen, After the Ball: How America Will Conquer Its Fear and Hatred of Gays in the '90s, New York: Doubleday, 1989.

# 13    *Same-sex marriage is simply wrong: the only valid marriage is between one man and one woman.*

**The Charge.** In seeking to distort and subvert the true purpose of the sexual act, one that is God-given, same-sex marriage violates natural law and the objective norms of morality.

It is true that the cause of gay marriage has recently scored some successes in a number of Western nations. We must steel ourselves to the prospect of further erosion of traditional marriage. Even a moderate like Sean Fieler, the president of Equinox Partners, a New York hedge fund, has expressed serious reservations. "The problem with gay marriage," he said, "is that it promotes a very harmful myth about the gay lifestyle. It suggests that gay relationships lend themselves to monogamy, stability, health and partnering in the same way heterosexual relationships do. That's not true." (*New York Times*, Jan. 30, 2013).

Commenting on the recent change of the law in England, Sir Roger Gale, a member of the House of Commons stated: "It is not possible to redefine marriage. Marriage is the union between a man and a woman; [it] has been historically, [and] remains so. It is Alice in Wonderland territory, Orwellian almost, for any government of any political persuasion to seek to come along and try to rewrite the lexicon.

It will not do." (Parliamentary debate of February 3, 2011.)

The state bestows numerous benefits on marriage for a good reason. By its very nature and design, traditional marriage provides the proper conditions for a stable, affectionate, and moral atmosphere that is beneficial to the upbringing of children—all fruit of the mutual affection of the parents. This aids in perpetuating the nation and strengthening society, an evident interest of the state. Homosexual "marriage" does not fosters such conditions. Its primary purpose, objectively speaking, is the personal gratification of two individuals whose union is sterile by nature. It is not entitled, therefore, to the protection that the state extends to true marriage.

**Background.** Whatever view one takes of it, the cause of same-sex marriage has made many advances in recent years. The introduction of same-sex marriage has varied by jurisdiction, resulting from legislative changes to marriage laws, court challenges based on constitutional guarantees of equality, or legalization by voters through referendums and ballot initiatives. That the recognition of same-sex marriages is a civil-rights issue has come to be accepted in many nations. Yet debates arise over whether same-sex couples should be allowed to enter into marriage, be required to use a different status (such as a civil union, which either grant equal rights as marriage or limited rights in comparison to marriage), or not have any such rights. Same-sex marriage can provide LGBT taxpayers with government services and make financial demands on them comparable to those afforded to and required of male-female married cou-

191

ples. Same-sex marriage also gives them legal protections such as inheritance and hospital visitation rights.

As of early 2013 eleven countries (Argentina, Belgium, Canada, Iceland, the Netherlands, Norway, Portugal, Spain, South Africa, and Sweden) permit same-sex couples to marry nationwide. Same-sex marriages are also performed and recognized in Mexico City, Quintana Roo, and parts of the United States. In Brazil civil unions may be converted into marriage. Some jurisdictions that do not perform same-sex marriages but recognize it being performed elsewhere include Israel, Aruba, Curaçao, and Sint Maarten, Rhode Island in the United States, Mexico, and Brazil. Australia recognizes same-sex marriages only if one partner has had gender reassignment therapy.

Some analysts state that financial, psychological and physical well-being are enhanced by marriage, and that children of same-sex couples benefit from being raised by two parents within a legally recognized framework supported by society's institutions. Court documents filed by American scientific associations also state that singling out gay men and women as ineligible for marriage both stigmatizes and invites public discrimination against them. The American Anthropological Association affirms that the finding of social-science research is clear: it does not support the view that either civilization or viable social order require the rejection of same-sex marriage.

*Response*. The view that marriage must be between one man and one woman has been abundantly discussed in recent years and found wanting. There is, for example, a great deal of cross-cultural evidence for polygamy. It is even found in the Bible. Clearly, then, the concept of marriage is not static; it evolves. Ar all events, then was then; now is now.

Some observers detect homophobia or heterosexism in the opposition to gay marriage. Significantly, the opposition has also been likened to past prohibitions of interracial marriage

The chief positive argument for same-sex marriage is one of equity. Why should one segment of the population be deprived of an advantage that is available to the majority? In fact access to same-sex marriage is increasingly defined as a basic human-rights issue. Moreover, it is generally conceded that marriage has many positive benefits, not just for the participants but also for society as a whole.

**BIBLIOGRAPHY**. Jonathan Rauch, Gay Marriage: Why It Is Good for Straights, and Good for America, New York: Times Books/Henry Holt, 2004; John Corvino and Maggie Gallagher, Debating Gay Marriage, New York: Oxford University Press, 2012.

# 14 *As a natural reaction, homosexuality elicits disgust. It is inherently repellent.*

*The Charge.* Many would subscribe to the following statement, a very moderate and reasonable one. "My reaction to homosexuality is personal and subjective; it is simply one of disgust and abhorrence. For that reason I think about the matter as little as possible. Perhaps I should not feel this way, but I do."

Some young people today are more forthright. When they say "no homo," they indicate that they want nothing to do with this behavior.

*Background.* Disgust is a type of aversive reaction that involves withdrawing from a person or object with strong expressions of revulsion, whether real or pretended. Another approach to disgust defines it as a defensive response guarding against potential contamination. In the view of some observers, disgust is a universal, basic emotion that functions to help protect an organism from ingesting potentially harmful substances, thereby promoting disease avoidance. It is is typically associated with things that are regarded as unclean, inedible, infections, gory, or otherwise offensive.

Fear of contamination, by insects, waste products, or any kind of rottenness and corruption, may inspire disgust. In this case, disgust arises from a process of inference from perceptual experience. For example, the understanding that

194

insects have, in the past, caused pestilence may lead to a present-moment extrapolation that certain other insects, however innocuous, are disgusting because they are causing, or could cause, disease.

Such analyses do not take into account cultural differences. For example, many Americans detest "stinky" French cheeses, which are nonetheless highly prized in that country. The reaction may also change over time. During the 1950s few Americans registered disgust when others smoked cigarettes. Now many do.

In the Hebrew Bible male homosexuality is condemned (in the book of Leviticus) as to'ebah, abomination. The abomination category embraces many forbidden things, including food taboos. Common to many of the objects of Scriptural disparagement, however various they may seem, is the idea of disgust.

Popular versions of the aversive reaction are still common. On September 7, 2011, the celebrity Paris Hilton reportedly remarked to a gay-male friend: "Ewww! Gay guys are the horniest people in the world. They're disgusting. Dude, most of them probably have AIDS. ... I would be so scared if I were a gay guy. You'll like, die of AIDS." Later Hilton apologized for the outburst.

Today some straight men report strong feelings of aversion when they perceive gay men making sexual overtures to them. In most cases these individuals remain unmollified when reminded of the fact that heterosexual men often "hit" on women in the same way. When they do it, it's

A-OK, but not when they receive such attentions.

**Response**. While homosexuality may inspire disgust in some individuals, it is not clear that it is inherently disgusting. In fact studies have shown that as individuals become aware of the homosexuality of close friends and family members the aversive reaction dissipates.

Martha Nussbaum, a legal theorist and ethicist, explicitly rejects disgust as an appropriate guide for legislation, arguing that the "politics of disgust" is an emotional gambit, not a rational argument. She maintains that the politics of disgust tends to reinforce bigotry in the form of sexism, homophobia, racism. and antisemitism.

Her 2004 book *Hiding From Humanity* examines the relationship of disgust and shame to a society's laws. She identifies disgust as a marker that bigoted, and often merely majoritarian, discourse employs to "put people in their place" by belittlement and disparagement, relegating them to the category of a despised minority. Taking the disgust ploy off the table would represent an important step towards achieving a humane and tolerant society.

**BIBLIOGRAPHY**. William Ian Miller, The Anatomy of Disgust, Cambridge, MA: Harvard University Press, 1998; Martha Nussbaum, Hiding From Humanity: Disgust, Shame, and the Law, Princeton: Princeton University Press, 2004; idem, From Disgust to Humanity: Sexual Orientation and Constitutional Law, New York: Oxford University Press, 2010.

# Part IV
# Personal and Psychological Factors

## 1  *Homosexuality is abnormal.*

***The Charge.*** Homosexual behavior is a prime example of abnormality. For that reason universities classify it under the rubric of abnormal psychology, a discipline addressing various types of pathology. To be sure, homosexuals should not be ridiculed or persecuted, but they must be encouraged honestly to acknowledge their plight and to seek the appropriate remedies.

That homosexuality is abnormal is a fact that is hard to dismiss. Moreover, it is not something that is just known to society itself but is well understood by the sufferers themselves. This inescapable reality has a particularly unfortunate effect on young people. According to Tony Perkins, president of the Family Research Council, a group fighting the spread of homosexuality in our society, gay and lesbian teens know very well that they are abnormal, and this awareness causes them to be depressed and even suicidal. This is no mere fantasy, for homosexuality is in fact abnormal, Perkins points out that kids know this, leading them to despair.

Today, by contrast, we hear much loose talk about homosexuality being "virtually normal." Yet this aberrant and destructive conduct cannot pass for normal, whether virtual or in any other fashion.

*Background*. If one uses the term abnormal in the statistical sense of "diverging from the middle range; unusual in terms of frequency," there is no doubt that homosexuals are in fact abnormal in our society. But then so are opera divas, arbitrageurs, and United States Senators.

Applied to social life, however, such an approach entails subjective judgments about what the good life is. Moreover, insofar as homosexual and other variant lifestyles can be considered "maladjusted," that assumption reflects the punitive intrusion of socially sanctioned proscriptions rather than any deficits stemming from the behavior itself. In other words, once the corrosive element of self-contempt, which is introjected by the social environment, is removed, homosexual men and lesbian women can function as well as anyone else.

Another difficulty with the concept is that the pair normal/abnormal suggests a sharp dichotomy: the one is totally different from the other. Alfred Kinsey's findings, however, suggest that sexual behavior is best understood as a continuum with many individuals falling between the poles and shifting positions over the course of their lives.

Two historical curiosities may be noted. In a harangue against sodomites, the French thirteenth-century poem *Le Roman de la Rose* (ll. 19619-20) refers to those who practice such *exceptions anormales*. In 1869 the Hungarian homo-

198

sexual theorist K. M. Kertbeny coined a word normalsexual (corresponding to our "heterosexual") to contrast with homosexual (which by inference is not normal). Kertbeny's first compound, in striking contrast to his second, did not catch on. Even so, today one sometimes finds the term "normals" casually deployed to designate straights, as if the label was unproblematic.

A close cousin of abnormal is anomaly. In modern times this term seems to have been first used in a sexual sense in the German form Anomalie by Richard von Krafft-Ebing in 1877. Etymologically, the noun represents the opposite of the Greek "omalos," meaning "even, level." (It is not derived from "anomos," "unlawful," though a link is often perceived.)

In 1927 a guilt-ridden British homosexual chose the pseudonym "Anomaly" for his book *The Invert.* (The writer's real name is not known.)

In 1991 the queer theorist Michael Warner popularized the term "heteronormativity," This term serves to characterize a presumably unwarranted privileging of heterosexuality as the only proper sexual orientation, In Warner's view it also serves to question the equation of gender differences with natural roles in life.

A related term is "homonormativity," defined as the absorption of heteronormative ideals and constructs into GLBT culture and individual identity. The term was popularized prominently by Lisa Duggan in 2003. However, Susan Stryker has noted its previous employment by transgender activists in the 1990s to decry the elevation of gay/lesbian norms over the concerns of trans people. Duggan holds that homonormativity fragments GLBT communities into hierarchies of worthiness. Ostensibly, GLBT people who come the closest to mimicking heteronormative standards of gender identity are deemed most worthy of receiving rights. Other individuals on the lower ranks of the hierarchy (transsexuals, transvestites, intersex individuals, bisexuals, and non-gender-identified persons) stand as an impediment to the status of this privileged class of homonormative individuals. Yet in protesting this presumed disparagement, the queer theorists fall into their own version of judgmentalism and condemnation.

*Response.* Generally speaking, to say that homosexuality is abnormal conveys a negative value judgment. It is bad. For this reason the term abnormal is insidious, as it enables the user to slide (usually unconsciously) from a statement of fact to a statement of value. It is precisely this impermissible slide that the philosopher David Hume warned us about long ago. But the misguided effort of trying to derive an "ought" from an "is" persists.

In the recent debate over gay marriage some opponents keep insisting that heterosexual marriage is "the norm," seeking once again to bridge the gap between is and ought. Some misconceptions never die.

Labeling whole groups of people abnormal in a pejorative sense is now generally recognized as biased and unhelpful. Most universities have abandoned catch-all courses in "abnormal psychology."

In keeping with recent developments in Queer Theory, it may be that everyone is "abnormal." In this case the term would lose its meaning, at least with reference to sexual orientation.

**BIBLIOGRAPHY**. Alfred Kinsey et al., "Normality and Abnormality in Sexual Behavior," in P. H. Hoch and J. Zubin, eds., Psychological Development in Health and Disease, New York: Grune and Stratton, 1949, 11-32; Andrew Sullivan, Virtually Normal: An Argument about Homosexuality, New York: Alfred A. Knopf, 1995.

# 2  *Homosexuality is perversion.*

***The Charge.*** Homosexual behavior ranks as a perversion for the following reason. The purpose of the sexual acts is to reproduce the species, a task that requires the partnership of a male and a female. Such couplings are preordained by nature. As with such other perversions as incest, bestiality, necrophilia, and pedophilia, same-sex conduct is unacceptable. According to the progay rationalizers, though, the homosexual object choice is determined from birth or in the early formative years. These people "cannot help it." Yet this claim does not pass muster. Could we not as easily say that pedophiles or persons who finds animals sexually attractive must be excused because they were simply born that way?

Today's ultrapermissive society looks on with a blind eye as people pick and choose their favorite perversions. At first sight some seem almost innocuous–or so we have been conditioned to believe. Yet when we allow one perversion, what is the next one to follow? We go down the proverbial slippery slope to perdition.

Today we confine pedophiles rather than merely sending them to seek psychological guidance or evaluation. Rightly we take child abusers out of circulation regardless of whether they were born that way or not, because we as a society deem that molesting a child is morally wrong and against the normal human psychic constitution.

In human conduct there is a correct path and an incorrect one. Those who choose the wrong path are justly termed "perverts" because they willfully depart from what they know is right in their heart of hearts.

**Background**. Perversion is a term that has been used historically to describe those types of human behavior that are perceived to be a departure from what is considered to be normal or orthodox.

In psychiatric usage the meaning stems mainly from the noted German sexologist Richard von Krafft-Ebing (1840-1902). This writer distinguished two categories of "perverse Handlungen," perverse (i.e. nonreproductive) sexual acts: 1) those motivated by Perversität (viciousness, depravity) and 2) manifestations of Perversion (a qualitative, pathological variation of the character of the sexual drive). Thus heterosexual fellatio would be the result of Perversität, while much homosexual activity would stem from Perversion.

Following a different trajectory, the French evolution of the idea was also complex, starting with the "déviations maladives de l'appetit vénérien" of Claude François Michéa (1849) and arriving at the "perversions sexuelles" of Valentin Magnan (1885).

The older meaning of perversion was nonsexual, implying a "deviation from the original meaning or doctrine," literally a "turning aside" from the norm. In Northern Europe in early modern times a "pervert" generally signified a heretic (as a Protestant who converted to Catholicism), the opposite of convert. Catholics returned the favor, referring to those who chose Protestantism as perverts.

Ever elusive, the definition and usage of the concept has shifted under the influence of such variables as period, person, religion, and culture. What some would describe as perversion, others might say is simply a variant form of human sexuality. In some cultures homosexuality once ranked as a perversion, and indeed still is in several; it is nevertheless widely seen in the western world today as a natural sexual variation.

In recent years several professional philosophers have attempted to reformulate the concept of perversion. Thomas Nagel, for example, argues that perversion is more psychological than physiological, and that perversions are "truncated or incomplete versions of the complete figuration." Thus bestiality, where there is lack of reciprocity, would be perversion, while homosexuality is not. Unfortunately, these philosophers' discussions are conducted in the afterglow of the earlier history of the set of terms - the adjectives perverse and perverted, the nouns perversity and perversion, and the verb to pervert - rendering problematic their intended reconstruction of it.

In early 2013 there are reports that the devotees of "kinky sex" (featuring bondage and domination) are seeking to rebrand the word pervert in much the same way that queer has been rebranded as a positive label - "pervert chic," in short.

*Response*. It is best to abandon such misleading terms. In fact, many professionals now prefer the expression paraphilia. This term refers to sexual arousal by objects, situations, or individuals that are not part of the normal range of

204

stimulation. The expression was introduced by the psycho-analyst Wilhelm Stekel in the 1920s. Later the American sexologist John Money popularized the term as a nonpejorative designation for unusual sexual interests. The concept is extremely broad; according to one enumeration there are 549 paraphilias. Typical examples include interactions with fetish objects (such as shoes and boots; soiled underwear; half-smoked cigars); animals; and nonconsenting partners. A peculiar example is "cleaning sex," where the individual derives erotic satisfaction from being allowed to clean another person's apartment.

At one time homosexuality was classified as a paraphilia. But clinicians no longer regard it as such. A 2012 literature study comparing homosexuality with paraphilias confirmed that homosexuality was sufficiently dissimilar from the paraphilias as to be considered an unrelated construct. In other words, same-sex behavior is not a paraphilia.

**BIBLIOGRAPHY**. Thomas Nagel, "Sexual Perversion," The Journal of Philosophy, 66:1 (1969), 5-17; Vernon A. Rosario, The Erotic Imagination: French Histories of Perversity, New York: Oxford University Press. 1997; American Psychiatric Association, Diagnostic and Statistical Manual of Mental Disorders, DSM-IV-TR. Washington, DC: American Psychiatric Association, 2000; Jesse Bering, Perv: The Sexual Deviant in All of Us, New York: Scientific American/FSG, 2013.

## 3 Homosexuality is inversion, involving the reversal of the sex roles that nature has assigned to human beings.

*The Charge*. Whether the cause is physiological or psychological, gay men typically identify as women and lesbians as men. Aptly, a male homosexual has been described as having a female soul in a male body. These people defy the norms of gender, something that is abhorrent to normal, decent people.

Despite pressure from gay-advocacy groups seeking to cover up this reality, the media sometimes get it right, as seen in the flamboyant and effeminate Jack McFarland on television's "Will and Grace" That character is much more believable than the "straight-appearing" nominal hero of the show, the attorney Will Truman. In the case of the butch lesbian Rosey O'Donnell, another media figure, her espousal of the traits of the opposite sex is plain to see. These supposed "stereotypes" are in fact true to life, validating the common-sense realism of the ordinary person over against the sophistry of self-appointed experts.

In keeping with their pathetic, effeminized state, gay men are inherently cowardly. The presence of these unmanly men constitutes a threat to any nation's military. Unfortunately, we in the United States have signally failed to attend to this principle. With the dismantling of Don't

206

Ask, Don't Tell, these sissies are now permitted, even encouraged to serve openly in our armed forces, undermining unit cohesion. Mannish lesbians pose a separate, but equally insidious threat.

***Historical Background.*** The pioneer in the struggle for homosexual rights Karl Heinrich Ulrichs (1824-1895) formulated the notion that the Urning, as he called the male individual attracted to his own sex, was endowed with *anima muliebris corpore virili inclusa*, "a female soul trapped in a male body." He took the notion from *Eros: die Männerliebe der Griechen* (Glarus and St. Gall, 1836-38) by Heinrich Hössli.

Ulrichs' formulation, strictly speaking, applies only to those sometimes termed "subject homoerotics" - individuals who feel themselves members of the opposite sex, playing the female role in relations with members of his own sex. As a scientific theory such a notion, because of the mind-body dualism which it entails, lacks scientific standing. Yet the reiteration of Ulrichs' views in the work of later homosexual writers helped to keep this meme alive into the twentieth century and beyond.

Some Hindus today explain male homosexuality by saying that the individual had previously lived as a woman.

The heyday of the clinical concept of inversion occurred in the closing decades of the nineteenth century when some medical and other writers stressed the link between homosexuality and inversion. For some, the term meant simply the reversal of the current of attraction from the opposite to one's own sex. Others believed that inversion entails also an adoption of patterns of thinking, feeling, and action that are characteristic of the other sex. In this broader sense it amounts to effeminacy in the male, and viraginousness in the female, but it would not include the majority of male homosexuals and lesbians who do not show these traits. Studies of androgyny have also suggested that there is a continuum rather than a sharp separation between the two poles of male and female, so that inversion in the sense of a complete volte-face does not seem to occur. In any event, the terms inversion and invert have acquired a negative, clinical aura, and for this reason they are less commonly used today.

An examination of the history of these terms is helpful in understanding the connotations they carry today. In 1878, in a professional article in the *Rivista di freniatria, di psichiatria e di medicina legale*, the Italian alienist Arrigo Tamassia introduced the term inversione, which was quickly adopted into other languages as well as Italian to render the cumbersome German expression die conträre Sexualempfindung which Karl Westphal had introduced in 1869. The new coinage owed its success not only to its grammatical malleability - yielding the noun invert and the adjective inverted - but also to the fact that while the word itself was new, the ideas on which it drew were deeply rooted in Western consciousness.

The byways of the history of ideas reveal many episodes of the use of the spatial metaphors of "backwards-to-forwards" and "upside down" to symbolize social abnormality. Sometimes the inversion procedure is temporal rather than spatial, as in reciting the alphabet or some ritual formula backwards to produce a magical spell.

In Euripides' play Medea (fifth century BCE), the social disturbance of role reversal catalyzed by the heroine's assumption of masculine qualities is evoked by the image of rivers running backwards in their course. And Orpheus, who according to some Greek sources invented pederasty, was supposed to have made wild oaks migrate from their mountain habitat to the seashore, and to reduce savage beasts to lamb-like docility, thus altering the natural order by switching things to their opposites. In Hellenistic times, the poet Sotades (third century BCE) invented a kind of verse which was innocuous when read forwards, but obscene backwards.

The sexual predilections of the Romans for the "posterior Venus" (anal receptivity) were held to be revealed in the very name Roma, which in reverse spells amor ("love"). In the Koran, God turns the sinful cities of Sodom and Gomorrah literally upside down. Medieval texts, such as the *Roman de la Rose*, speak of sodomites doing things à rebours ("in reverse"), an expression that served Joris-Karl Huysmans in 1884 as the title for his novel of aristocratic perversion. Sixteenth- and seventeenth-century Europe witnessed the popularity of a genre of popular prints known as Le Monde à l'Envers or The World Upside Down, wherein alongside such outlandish things as fish nesting in trees and men plowing the sea, we find the wife going out to hunt while the husband stays home to mind the baby, and similar instances of sex-role reversal.

As used by late nineteenth-century writers, the word in-

209

version often had an application that went beyond sexual orientation. The medical authorities who studied "inversion" were fascinated by gender-role reversal - masculine women and feminine men - positing such purportedly biological tendencies as the root cause of "inverted" sexual object choice, rather than vice versa. Certain writers preferred to restrict the term to the narrower meaning of the reversal of the secondary sexual characters as distinct from the sexual orientation proper; thus only the effeminate homosexual and the butch lesbian were "inverts" in this sense.

The idea was used in a number of creative ways by Marcel Proust in his great novel sequence *A la recherche du temps perdu* (1913-27) which shows that it need not always be negative. One of his homosexual characters, Robert de Saint-Loup, seeks out danger in battle instead of fleeing it, while Baron Charlus becomes more pro-German rather than less so as war nears. In a larger sense the novel's goal - the gradual recovery of more and more layers of memory - is a subtle process of inversion or retrogression. This great enterprise is mirrored in Proust's fascination with musical techniques, including the device of melodic inversion.

*Response*. Popular versions of the idea linger in the notion that gay men are "really" women and lesbians are "really" men. In fact some young people do adopt the clothing and mannerisms of the opposite sex. This is a common feature of the coming-out process, which most grow out of. Others, however, continue and are commonly termed transgendered. Such individuals have long enjoyed prestige in the world of entertainment. Recent advances in understanding

210

have made the lives of these persons easier.

Still, there is no reason to equate this gender-bending with homosexuality per se. Indeed, many transgender people deny that they are gay or lesbian.

In these days of growing acceptance of trans people, it seems more and more understandable that some individuals will choose not to accept conventional views of gender roles. These choices must be respected and not subjected to pejorative labeling.

The idea that gay men are unsuitable for military service is disproved by the numerous cases of successful gay warriors, from Alexander the Great and the Theban Band to Eugene of Savoy and General Friedrich Wilhelm von Steuben, a Revolutionary War hero.

**BIBLIOGRAPHY**. Tom Bergling, Sissyphobia: Gay Men and Effeminate Behavior, New York: Southern Tier Editions, 2001.

# 4   *Same-sex behavior is simply a preference.*

*The Charge.* Homosexuals could be just like the rest of us if they would only make the effort. Instead they willfully embrace deviance and self-indulgence. Adding insult to injury, in daily life they increasingly affect blatant displays of their affliction - what they call "gay and proud." Surely they must realize that exhibitions of this behavior are distasteful to the majority. Such flaunting of their moral deficits does not help their cause.

By far the best course would be for these unfortunates to cease their perversion altogether. This is simply a matter of will power. As Jonathan I. Katz, a professor at Washington University in St. Louis, remarked in a 2003 blog post, "What of those cursed with unnatural sexual desires? Must they forever suppress these desires? Yes, but this is hardly a unique fate. Almost everyone has desires which must be suppressed. Most men and women think adulterous thoughts fairly often, and find themselves attracted to members of the opposite sex to whom they are not married. Morality requires them to suppress these desires, and most do not commit adultery, though they feel lust in their hearts. Almost everyone, at one time or another, covets another's property. They do not steal. Many people feel great anger or intense hatred at some time in their lives. They do not kill."

*Background.*   Sociologists   and   economists   have

212

advanced several types of preference theory. For example, the American economist Paul Samuelson has advocated what he terms revealed preference theory as a method for comparing the influence of advertising on consumer behavior. The models assume that the preferences of consumers can be ascertained by their purchasing habits.

Sexual object choice is not like trying to decide which brand of toothpaste to buy. Still, the term sexual preference finds some favor among those who hold that sexuality is fluid and incorporates an element of choice, as opposed to those who believe sexuality is fixed early in life.

The queer theorist Judith Butler espouses a related concept. In her 1990 book *Gender Trouble*, she posits a performative or elective understanding of gender, as opposed to the idea that gender manifestations express some sort of innate or natural gender. Butler holds that the performance of gender actually creates gender. She compares the enactment of gender to a theatrical presentation.

*Response.* If homosexuality is a mere preference, then heterosexuality must be also. Yet we see few, if any exhortations that those who suffer from this failing must change. It would not be easy to do so–in fact almost impossible. The same is true with homosexuality.

In fact, the expression "sexual preference" finds favor among those who have unrealistic expectations about the malleability of orientation and its expression, and who seek to alter its character–that is, if the orientation is of the "wrong sort."

If sexual orientation were simply a preference one could switch it just as one shifts from cheeseburgers to steak or from blue jeans to a tuxedo. Some efforts at "curing" homosexuality rely on a version of this model. Since the theory is inadequate, the interventions have generally failed.

Today the expression "sexual orientation" is rightly dominant, emphasizing that erotic attraction emanates from the deep structure of the personality. It is not a mere choice, taste, or whim which can be easily altered. Nor can the desires be simply suppressed by an act of will power.

However, there is some earlier history of speaking of homosexuality as a taste. Correspondingly, in French it could be called a *goût*. This French term retains some popularity today, at least in Francophone areas, where the idea can be used to refer to particular inclination, as for hirsute or smooth bodies, muscular or slender ones, and so forth. But sexual orientation itself is different from these specifics, because it is experienced as part of one's core personality.

# 5   Instead of maintaining a low profile, as decency requires, homosexuals are prone to extravagant displays of excess and exhibitionism.

*The Charge.* Discretion is definitely not part of the gay repertoire. These reprobates get a thrill out of what they term "camping up a storm," engaging in flamboyant conduct that is designed to offend. Displays of this misbehavior are particularly egregious during the "gay-pride" events that blight many cities in June of each year.

Homosexuals would be well advised not to advertise their all-too-obvious affliction. Adopting an aggressive approach only brings disapproval, It is antithetical to the very acceptance these individuals claim to be seeking, which can only be earned (if in fact it can be) through a modest demeanor. Exuberance and self-indulgence retard their progress in integrating with polite society,

*Background.* For generations, concealment and discretion, the closet in short, represented the unspoken rule for gay people - a basic survival strategy. Paradoxically, though, in earlier years some "obvious" or stereotypical gays defiantly embraced the opposite tactic of exhibitionism. They excelled in a sort of performance in public places, involving exaggerated gestures, high-pitched shrieking, and mock femininity. Such gambits were known as camping up a storm, flaming (also "sending up flares"), and screaming (as in "screaming queens"). Dropping pins meant to proclaim one's feminine side.

What is one to make of these labels? These slang expressions served to signal disapproval on the part of the more reticent members of the community who feared the negative consequences of the provocation. Yet those who engaged in the behavior took a different view, regarding it as a necessary safety valve. The conduct might also have been intended as a way of calling out straight society for its hypocrisy. Some flaming may have been involuntary, however.

Popular usage has detected a particular character type here, a social role that persists to this day. A drama queen is a histrionic gay man who relishes his capacity to "make scenes." Typically, the outbursts show a kind of exaggerated patter that resembles the recitatives and arias of opera. The affinity of gay men for the theater and the opera has often been noted. Still, it is not necessary to be a fan of those art forms to qualify as a drama queen.

Such provocation was not always simply a manifestation of personal idiosyncrasy. The joyous exuberance of the gay-liberation movement of the 1970s represented a positive channeling of collective exhibitionism. Utilizing zaps, confrontation, and in-your-face tactics, gay activists of the 1970s pioneered in repurposing such impulses as creative tools for advancing social change. During the following decade AIDS activists, especially those in the organization ACT-UP specialized in positive uses of confrontation. To-

216

day, with many of the key goals accomplished, the need for such interventions is less keenly felt.

The first gay-pride parade was held in New York City in June of 1970. The custom has since spread around the world, from San Francisco to Berlin and from Mauritius to São Paolo. These events attract a large variety of participants, including some flamboyant individuals, some of them deliberately provocative.

As a result, there is opposition to pride events both within the GLBT and mainstream populations. Some gay and lesbian critics charge the parades with an undue emphasis on sex and fetishism which they view as counterproductive to GLBT interests, exposing the larger gay community to ridicule. GLBT activists counter that mainstream media have played a negative role in featuring the most outlandish and therefore non-representative aspects of the community. This fact serves to play into the hands of exhibitionists who are encouraged to adopt ever-more-flamboyant costumes in order to gain media coverage.

For their part, social conservatives decry such events because they view them to be contrary to public morality. This belief focuses on certain elements typically found in the parades, such as public nudity, BDSM paraphernalia, and other sexualized features. Within the academic community, there has been criticism that the parades actually tend to strengthen the homosexual-heterosexual divide. Unintentionally, they may serve to advance the essentialist view that GLBT people are totally different from "normals."

Apart from public display, excess may also occur in one's lifestyle. Some gay men have had thousands of sexual partners, and boast of their numerous conquests, which are generally anonymous. As a rule, though, these sexual athletes do not regard their exploits as excess, but as a natural expression of the male erotic drive. Some individuals of this type are oncers, who boast of never having had sex twice with the same person. The circuit parties, so popular in the 1990s, combined indulgence in drugs with anonymous sex. All these things reflect sectors of the gay-male community, but are not representative of the whole.

*Response.* Some kinds of excess, at least those that bring health problems, should be avoided. However, almost all human beings have a basic need for expressivity. And sometimes this requirement entails "letting go." As long as no one is harmed by this conduct and no laws are broken, there are no grounds for alarm,

**BIBLIOGRAPHY**. Lynda Johnson, Queering Tourism: Paradoxical Performances at Gay Pride Parades, London: Routledge, 2005.

# 6 Some gay people demonstrate a corrosive negativity, internalizing the stereotypes that are deployed against them.

*The Charge.* Homosexuals never cease to complain about the stereotypes they claim are imposed on them. Yet sometimes they embrace these stereotypes themselves. In this way, they arrogate to themselves a prerogative - entertaining homonegative stereotypes - that they would deny to others. Something similar is found in the negative language used by black rappers. But again, some thoughtful critics have taken exception to this mode.

*Background.* This phenomenon has sometimes been termed abjection. We normally think of homophobic tropes as ones generated by the host society, even as they are resisted by the victims. In some cases, though, the subjects internalize the stereotypes, manifesting various distorted and abject attitudes and modes of behavior as a consequence. As a form of self-inferiorization abjection is the reverse of the medal of disparagement by others.

Gays have internalized these hostile themes in various ways. In extreme cases the embrace of negativity may amount to self-hatred, what is sometimes termed internalized homophobia. In other instances the reception may be more playful, even constituting (according to some) a form of resistance. Some say that in adopting such epithets as queer, gay users are "taking back" the terms. There are limits to the applicability of this principle. During the sexual revolution of the 1970s a few radical gay men insisted on labeling themselves cocksuckers, recommending that others do the same. While most gay men have engaged in fellatio from time to time, it seems inappropriate to make this our defining concept. The argument would be similar if women, say, were joyously to call themselves sluts. Of course most don't.

Expressed verbally, the phenomenon of abjection normally plays out on a much less theoretical and more mundane plane. In the appropriate context, embrace of a whole range of terms, from degenerate and anomaly to faggot and homo, can constitute abjection. But what is the appropriate context. One useful distinction is between the inner and outer situations. That is to say, use of such a term in a closed setting in which only other gay people are present does not amount to abjection. That is the "inner" situation. The outer one occurs when the speaker presents himself to a heterosexual audience as an exemplar of inferiorization. A similar phenomenon occurs with African Americans, who feel authorized to use the n- word among themselves in certain contexts, but object when it becomes overt in largely white contexts.

Some terms become detoxified over time. For example, in Britain one might refer to someone as "you old bugger!" without implying any real disparagement. That is because the word bugger, which possessed a powerful negative charge in the middle ages and the early modern period, has since lost it in the British Isles—-even though buggery was a statutory offense until 1967.

There are several other gray areas. Once taboo, the term queer is now accepted in many circles. The pink triangle reflects a color patch the Nazis required homosexual inmates of their concentration camp to wear. It might be thought that the adoption of this symbol by gay-rights advocates in recent decades reflects the abjection principle. This does not seem to be so, though, and in these cases we may have a successful instance of detoxification. S/M, camp flamboyance, and other dramatizing activities are probably not examples of abjection.

In addition to verbal embrace of the abjection principle, such behavior exists on the plane of action. This is the matter of so-called self-destructive conduct. Here again one must be careful. The accusation of self-destruction appeals to heterosexuals who view the "homosexual lifestyle" as itself self-destructive.

Still, most would agree that the bug chasers who for a time deliberately sought to contract HIV were self-damaging; this is an extreme form of abjection. It now seems to be uncommon.

*Response.* Clearly the concept of abjection has some explanatory value, but it seems confused because is hard to establish clear boundaries. There remains the issue of those members of minority groups who internalize the hurtful stereotypes that have been used against them.

**BIBLIOGRAPHY**. Barry D. Adam, The Survival of Domination: Inferiorization and Everyday Life, New York: Elsevier, 1978; Julia Kristeva, Powers of Horror: An Essay on Abjection, New York: Columbia University Press, 1982.

# 7 *A homosexual orientation typically develops in a family situation in which the mother is too attentive or "close binding," while the father is aloof or absent.*

*The Charge.* Young people who are destined to become homosexual have the misfortune to be brought up in dysfunctional families. To be sure, overly protective mothers in these families are well intentioned. For their part, the fathers often practice benign neglect. The combination of the two attitudes creates a homosexual neurosis that must be addressed by therapy.

*Background.* In recent decades, the chief advocate of this view was the psychoanalyst Irving Bieber (1909-1989), who believed that homosexuality was an illness that must be cured.

In 1962 Bieber headed a team of colleagues that published *Homosexuality: A Psychoanalytical Study of Male Homosexuals* (Basic Books), a nine-year study of 106 gay men. The study maintained that disruptions in family relationships early in life contributed to a child's homosexual development. It concluded: "A constructive, supportive, warmly related father precludes the possibility of a homosexual son; he acts as a neutralizing, protective agent should the mother make seductive or close-binding attempts."

Critics have pointed out that many heterosexual men grew up in similar families, so that a homosexual outcome was not inevitable or typical. For a long time, American culture favored a style of fatherhood that was strong but aloof. As far as the qualities of the mother are concerned, who is to say when the mother is "too loving?" Such judgments are inherently subjective.

The Bieber theory was originally developed to reflect conditions in the United States, especially our family structure. Yet different family structures prevail in other parts of the world. The prominence of gay people has been documented in Japan, India, Thailand, Brazil, South Africa and countless other societies. The Bieber concept of etiology cannot account for these people.

*Response.* The original theory, which sought to blame the mother, surely reflects the misogyny endemic in our society. One should think carefully about the effects of this tendency.

Even though the Bieber theory is generally discounted among clinicians and other professionals nowadays, uneasiness persists among some parents. They torture themselves by asking: Did I "make" my child homosexual by poor parenting?

Fortunately an excellent organization exists to help parents and others cope as they learn of the sexual orientation of their children. This is Parents, Families and Friends of Lesbians and Gays (PFLAG), an organization of family members and friends of GLBT people, PFLAG has more than 350 affiliates throughout the United States, the District of Columbia, Puerto Rico, and 11 other countries. The organization was founded in New York City in April of 1972 by Jeanne Manford, mother of the noted gay activist Morty Manford.

# 8 Typically, homosexuals are given to complaining and grudge gathering.

**The Charge.** In 1971 the psychoanalyst Edmund Bergler reported his finding that male homosexuals are typically characterized by "injustice collecting, fault-finding, and accumulation of resentments."

Instead of courageously accepting the ills that their choice of a deviant lifestyle inevitably brings, homosexuals are constantly whining and complaining. This unpleasant trait alienates those who would seek to help them.

**Background.** In daily life all sorts of people complain - about such things as not having enough money, harassment at the work place. and intractable health problems. These are legitimate issues. Yet some individuals seem to be given to whining without a cause. There is no "objective correlative" for their misery. It has been claimed that homosexuals belong to this pattern.

The Vienna, then New York, psychoanalyst Edmund Bergler (1899-1962) developed the theory that the basic neurosis is psychic masochism, and that homosexuals are neurotic "injustice collectors." In Bergler's view the provocative behavior observed in his patients arises in the following manner. They create a situation in which some substitute for the mother of early childhood is perceived as "refusing." Not realizing that they are themselves to blame, they become aggressive in righteous indignation and self-defense alternating with self-pity, while "unconsciously enjoying psychic masochism." Under the facade of pseudo-aggression are hidden deep self-damaging tendencies. The psychic masochist in the homosexual "habitually transforms conscious displeasure into unconscious pleasure," so that he can resign himself to the punishments resulting from the humiliation and insult heaped on him by an intolerant society. Instead of learning to avoid punishment, the homosexual actually enjoys it, and by turning displeasure into pleasure he "takes the sting out of the pain and defeat of his tormented existence." Such were Bergler's idiosyncratic views.

*Response.* While it is true that a homosexual with self-damaging tendencies (and such people do exist) is likely to encounter reprisals from a society permeated with homophobia, only a shrinking minority of homosexuals are of this type. Moreover, early writers denying the pathological character of homosexuality pointed to the success with which many closeted homosexuals deceive intolerant heterosexuals in their entourage with the skill of an accomplished undercover agent or spy.

Paradoxically, the "injustice collector" mentality may also have had the function of preserving the individual's self-esteem in the face of society's condemnation and rejection. Instead of internalizing the values of the homophobic culture, he can in effect say: "You are the wrongdoer, and I am the one to whom the injustice is being done." The alternative would be to accept the stigma of being a sinner, a criminal, and a monster - which a rational subject

227

could scarcely do without a total loss of self-respect. Whatever therapeutic results Bergler scored with his homosexual analysands seem to have been with individuals whose superego had been unable to ward off society's castigation of their behavior and the ensuing guilt and self-reproach. Then his very success with them attracted ever more to his couch, so that his "patient universe" became skewed in the direction of such guilt-ridden personalities.

In the closing decades of the twentieth century, the notion that complaining was particularly characteristic of minorities gave way as all sorts of groups, from African Americans to women, came forward with similar grievances. These grievances were (and in many cases still are) all too real. While this assertive tendency has been derided as "Victimology 101," it was probably a necessary stage of evolution of these groups as they have propelled themselves towards self-respect and self-assertion.

One could anticipate that such complaining would decline as society began to relinquish its policies of discrimination and defamation of these groups. And so it has.

**BIBLIOGRAPHY**. Edmund Bergler, "The Myth of a New National Disease: Homosexuality and the Kinsey Report," Psychiatric Quarterly, 22 (1948), 66-88; idem, The Basic Neurosis: Oral Regression and Psychic Masochism, New York: Grune and Stratton, 1949; Edmund Bergler and Joost A. M. Meerloo, "The Injustice Collector," in Justice and Injustice, New York: Grune and Stratton, 1963, p. 20 ff.

# 9   *The homosexual lifestyle is a manifestation of immaturity.*

*The Charge.*   In a 2008 interview, Pastor Rick Warren observed, "You say because I have natural impulses to the same sex, I shouldn't have to rein them in. Well I disagree. I think that's part of maturity. I think that's part of delayed gratification; I think that's part of character."

All too frequently, gay men remain perpetual adolescents frolicking in sensual indulgence, while disdaining the adult responsibility that comes from the challenge of forming stable families. Some gay people are honest enough to acknowledge this failing, but not many.

*Background.*   The locus classicus of the idea of homosexual immaturity appears in the influential writings of Sigmund Freud. Starting with an a priori assumption of a natural "procreative instinct," Freud set forth a fanciful theory of psychosexual development in which a male infant passes through narcissistic, oral, anal and phallic stages, attaining an Oedipal desire to have sex with his mother. Then fearing castration by his jealous father, the maturing male transfers his love to another woman. In this way the goal, the only acceptable one, is achieved: a glorious heterosexuality.

Men become homosexual, Freud thought, when this progression is inhibited—-he never explains how–and the individual remains fixated at some preliminary stage ofdevelopment. In this way the sufferer undergoes one of several fates. He is blocked at a narcissistic stage, or fails to negotiate the Oedipal phase, or fears castration by a woman's vagina.

Odd as all this seems, the result was that homosexuals were viewed as psychosexually immature. In his 1933 *New Introductory Lectures on Psychoanalysis* Freud wrote that homosexuals "have failed to accomplish some part of normal sexual development." And in his 1935 "Letter to an American Mother," (published in 1951) Freud wrote, "We consider (homosexuality) to be a variation of the sexual function produced by a certain arrest of sexual development."

In simplified form Freud's ideas migrated to America. In a notorious 1980 essay entitled "The Boys on the Beach," conservative writer Midge Decter explained that for homosexuals there were: "No households of wives and children requiring security; no entailments of school bills, doctor and dentist bills; no lifetime of acquiring the goods needed for family welfare and the goods desired for family entertainment, with a margin left over for that greatest of all heterosexual entailments, the Future: no such households burdened the overwhelmingly vast majority of homosexuals." Male homosexuality, Decter claimed, is a flight from adult responsibility "far more than a wholehearted embrace of men."

Earlier, in January 1948, the writer Anais Nin had confessed similar misgivings. "[W]hat I see in the homosexual is different from what others see. I never see perversion, but rather a childlike quality, a pause in childhood or adolescence when one hesitates to enter the adult world. The re-

230

lationship based on identification, on twinship, or 'the double,' on narcissism, is a choice more facile and less exigent than that between men and women.... There was often a parody, too, of parents or grandparents, an attachment to the past (love of antiques), always a fixation on preadolescence, when our sexual inclinations are not yet crystallized, and always some traumatic event which caused fear of women, hence the hatred of her." Further, "[W]enever I came close to a homosexual, what I found was childishness."

Now these ideas, in their Freudian guise, have been embraced by the magisterium of the Catholic church. The gravamen of the 2005 Vatican Instruction on sexuality reads (in paragraph four): "The candidate to the ordained ministry, therefore, must reach affective maturity. Such maturity will allow him to relate correctly to both men and women..." "Affective maturity" is not defined but since "affective" refers to feelings or emotions the term refers to emotional maturity, specifically here sexual emotions.

Then paragraphs 8 and 9 state that "those who ... present deep-seated homosexual tendencies ... find themselves in a situation that gravely hinders them from relating correctly to men and women." So although the Instruction avoids saying so explicitly, gay men are barred from priesthood training because they are thought to have immature sexual feelings. It is curious that the ghost of Sigmund Freud should have insinuated itself into Vatican thinking at this late date. Yet that seems to be what has happened.

Either through trickle-down or spontaneous generation some of these ideas have appeared in popular consciousness.

It is not unusual for parents, noting the same-sex proclivities of their adolescent children, to make remarks such as the following; "It's only a phase," or "(S)he will grow out of it." This expectation seems more common with homosexual women than men, hence the expression LUG ("lesbian until graduation"), to designate a female college student who will ostensibly settle into regular, heterosexual life. Also found is "hasbian."

Religious groups seek to "rescue" homosexuals from their supposed self-destructive immaturity, by turning them into ex-gays.

Inadvertently perhaps, some gay men seem inclined to confirm the immaturity stereotype through open displays of frivolity. Such indulgences range from flamboyant behavior to an obsessive concern with gossip and popular culture. These traits may be accompanied by disorientation, produced by stimulants or an irregular lifestyle: hence the term dizzy queen. For some the word gay itself encapsulates these notions. In this censorious view homosexuals lack a tragic sense of life, a deficiency possibly rooted in their tendency to avoid family responsibilities.

In the popular mind, homosexuals are regarded as excessively hedonistic, and preoccupied with sex. It may be that the term homosexual itself serves to bolster this stereotype. For that reason, LGBT or queer may be better terms.

*Response.* In recent years, sociologists have long recognized the human need for play - the ludic element - in maintaining a sense of humanity and balance. There is no

232

valid reason why this harmless outlet should be denied to LGBT people.

**BIBLIOGRAPHY**. Kenneth Lewes, Psychoanalysis and Male Homosexuality, new ed., New York: Jason Aronson, 2009.

# 10 *Homosexuals are morbidly obsessed with sex.*

*The Charge.* While normal people assign to sex a subordinate place in their lives, homosexuals make it central and obsessive. Put simply, they are sex addicts.

*Background.* In so far as gay people have been defined according to their sexual object choices, it is natural for them to place sex high on their list of defining characteristics. The word homosexual itself tends to reinforce this perception.

In addition, the marginality to which gay people have been restricted tends to make them more adventurous. and this adventurousness extends into sexual practices.

These factors have fed the common stereotype that gay men are promiscuous and are either unwilling or unable to forge enduring or long-term relationships. Yet several surveys of gay men in the United States have shown that between 40% and 60% are involved in a steady relationship, and that many others are single, but have the intention of becoming involved only in monogamous relationships.

Research also suggests that lesbians may be somewhat more likely than gay men to be in steady relationships. In terms of unprotected sex, a 2007 study by Goudreau and Golden cited two large population surveys as showing that "the majority of gay men had similar numbers of unprotected sexual partners annually as straight men and women."

Another persistent stereotype associated with the male homosexual community is partying. Before the Stonewall Riots in 1969, most GLBT people were extremely private and closeted, and house parties and, later, bars and taverns became, exceptionally, places where they could meet, socialize, and feel safe. The riots greatly enhanced the modern LGBT social movement and acceptance of sexual and gender minorities has steadily increased since. Generally festive and party-like social occasions remain important for organizing and fundraising in the GLBT community. In cities where there are large concentrations of GLBT people benefit events and bar fundraisers are still common. Ushered in by underground gay clubs and disc jockeys, the disco era at the end of the last century kept the "partying" aspect vibrant and ushered in the more hardcore circuit-party movement, hedonistic and associated with controlled substances.

The broader background is that, historically, gay people have had few family ties, freeing them for recreational activities. Yet these are not restricted to sexual pursuits, but include travel and an interest in music and the arts.

*Response.* The growing popularity of gay marriage indicates that gay people are seeking stability, just like everyone else. As this pattern becomes more general, they will be less promiscuous.

In fact lesbians have always been inclined to form stable coupled relationships, and now gay men are following their lead. Adoption or parenting by surrogates works to create real families headed by gay people. This factor makes them less concerned with sex.

**BIBLIOGRAPHY**. Karla Jay and Allen Young, The Gay Report: Lesbians and Gay Men Speak Out about Sexual Experiences and Lifestyles, New York: Summit. 1979; Stephen M. Goudreau and Matthew R. Golden, "Biological and Demographic Causes of High HIV and Sexually Transmitted Disease Prevalence in Men Who Have Sex with Men, "Sexually Transmitted Infections", 83:6 (October 2007), 458-62.

# 11  *Homosexuality is shameful.*

*The Charge.* Sometimes gay and lesbian people are honest enough to recognize what others know full well. What they are doing is manifestly wrong.

They should be ashamed of themselves!

*Background.* Overlapping with guilt and embarrassment, shame remains a somewhat elusive concept. In his 1872 book *The Expression of the Emotions in Man and Animals*, Charles Darwin described the affect of shame as consisting of blushing, confusion of mind, eyes cast downward, slack posture, and lowered head. He believed that the experience of shame was a world-wide phenomenon, one that was not limited to any particular culture. It was a human universal.

Yet cultural anthropologists take a different view, stressing two different situations. They identify shame societies (also termed honor-shame cultures) as ones in which the primary device for gaining control over children and maintaining social order is the inculcation of shame and the accompanying threat of ostracism. Traditional China and Japan often figure as typical instances of shame societies. In this view a shame society contrasts with a guilt society where control is maintained by creating and continually reinforcing the feeling of guilt (and the expectation of punishment either in the present or in the afterlife) with regard to certain condemned behaviors.

Western societies are often regarded as guilt societies. Probably this contrast is too stark, for shame and guilt seem to occur almost everywhere.

A "sense of shame" is a common way of speaking of the consciousness or awareness of shame as a state or condition. Such cognition may result from the experience of the shame affect or, more generally, may stem from any situation of embarrassment, dishonor, disgrace, inadequacy, humiliation, or chagrin.

"To shame" generally means actively to assign or communicate a state of shame to another. Maneuvers designed to uncover or expose the infractions sometimes serve this purpose, as are imprecations like "Shame!" or "Shame on you!" More covertly, gossip plays a role.

To "have shame" means to maintain a sense of restraint against offending others (as with modesty, humility, and deference), while to "have no shame" is to behave recklessly without such restraint (as with excessive pride or hubris).

Finally, the expression "that's a shame," means that the speaker recognizes events or situations as real, but deplorable.

In December of 1894 Lord Alfred Douglas, Oscar Wilde's protégé, published the following poem in *The Chameleon*, a literary magazine:

Last night unto my bed bethought there came
Our lady of strange dreams, and from an urn

She poured live fire, so that mine eyes did burn
At the sight of it. Anon the floating fame
Took many shapes, and one cried: "I am shame
That walks with Love, I am most wise to turn
Cold lips and limbs to fire; therefore discern
And see my loveliness, and praise my name."

And afterwords, in radiant garments dressed
With sound of flutes and laughing of glad lips,
A pomp of all the passions passed along
All the night through; till the white phantom ships
Of dawn sailed in. Whereat I said this song,
"Of all sweet passions Shame is the loveliest."

For a long time this manifestation of gay self-contempt–
shame– received little formal attention. At least it was neglected in public gay and lesbian circles. But recently a
change has occurred.

Starting in 1998, Gay Shame was a movement emerging
from a sector within the GLBT community that presented
itself as a radical alternative to gay mainstreaming. Proponents sought to confront the established view of gay pride,
ostensibly marred by commercialization and corporate spon-
sorship. They attacked "queer assimilation," appearing in
what they perceived as oppressive and conservative societal
structures.

Observances of Gay Shame began in 1998 with an event
in Brooklyn, New York. *Swallow Your Pride* was a zine
published by the people involved in planning Gay Shame
in New York. Three issues were released. The movement

later spread to San Francisco, Toronto, London, and Sweden. Currently, the trend seems to be ebbing.

In March 2003 an academic conference occurred on the theme at the University of Michigan at Ann Arbor. The gathering saw friction between the activists and the academics, growing out of differences in strategy, and the activists' charge that the academics didn't do enough to acknowledge their power and class privilege, and to share more of their bounty with the activists.

Somewhat confusingly, the 2004 Gay Shame event was billed as "Now in its 9th great year." The observance included performance art and queer-bash make-overs. It was billed as "The Annual Festival of Homosexual Misery." Purportedly, the 2009 event was the last. This does not seem to be quite true. On Saturday, November 24, 2012, a small Gay Shame event occurred at the Modern Times Bookstore in San Francisco. Still this is a trend whose time came - and went.

*Response.* The Gay Shame movement attested the way in which some GLBT people will seek to "detoxify" homonegative motifs and use them for their own purposes. In this case the effort seems to have failed.

# 12  *In order to obtain an erotic thrill, some homosexuals are prone to insert gerbils into the rectum.*

*The Charge.* Homosexuals are anally fixated. They derive pleasure from inserting foreign objects into the rectal cavity, including dildos, vegetables, and - most notoriously - the small animals known as gerbils.

In terms of Freudian psychoanalysis, such activities constitute a regression to the anal stage of human psychic development. Mature individuals have no need to avail themselves of such dangerous gratification.

*Background.* Gerbiling, also known as gerbil stuffing or gerbil shooting, is an urban legend designating a supposed sexual practice of inserting small live animals (usually gerbils but also mice, hamsters, rats and various other rodents) into the human rectum to obtain stimulation. Some variations of the legend suggest that the practitioner might be inclined to douse the rodent with a narcotic substance such as cocaine prior to the insertion.

An urban legend (also known as an urban myth, urban tale, or contemporary legend) is a form of modern folklore consisting of stories that may or may not have been believed by their tellers to be true. As with all folklore and mythology, the designation makes no judgment regarding the story's veracity, but merely attests that it is in circulation, shows variation over time, and carries some significance that induces the community to preserve and propagate it.

Despite the name, an urban legend does not necessarily originate in an urban area. Rather, the term is used to differentiate modern legends from the body of traditional folklore stemming from preindustrial times.

Urban legends sometimes appear in news stories and, in recent years, they have circulated via e-mail and the social media. Those who repeat them commonly allege that such occurrences happened to a "friend of a friend"- so often, in fact, that "friend of a friend" ("FOAF") has become a common designation for such narratives.

Some hardy urban legends have passed through the years with only minor changes to suit regional conditions. One example is the bizarre tale of a woman killed by spiders nesting in her elaborate hairdo. More recent legends tend to reflect modern circumstances, including the story of victims ambushed, anesthetized, and waking up minus one kidney, which was surgically removed for sale as a transplant (a story folklorists refer to as "The Kidney Heist").

With regard to gay men, the gerbiling legend derives some surface plausibility because of the practice of some individuals of inserting inanimate objects, such as dildos and various fruits and vegetables, into the rectum. More dangerous are small bottles and light bulbs. As early as 1857 the French physician Ambroise Tardieu cited a number of medical reports of small bottles and drinking glasses that had been recovered from the rectal cavities of those seeking gratification in this way (*Etude Médico-Légale sur les*

*Attentats aux Mœurs,* first ed., Paris, 1857).

This practice is a form of autoeroticism, usually performed solo, though not always. The behavior occurs among all sorts of people, not just gay men. Tardieu mentioned, for example, a case of a French husband who had inserted a bottle in the anus of his wife.

The inserted objects noted above are the usual ones. It is quite another matter, however, to suggest that this practice involves living creatures. One case, of uncertain authenticity, reputedly involved an eel.

According to folklorist Jan Harold Brunvand, accounts of gerbiling were first recorded in 1984, and initially were said to involve a mouse and an unidentified man. In subsequent versions of the story, the animal was a gerbil and the story was ascribed to several male celebrities.

For some reason, the most popular victim of this unsubstantiated gossip has been the actor Richard Gere. The legend has clung to Gere's name since at least the mid-1980s, when he was still married to Cindy Crawford. Supposedly the star was admitted for an emergency "gerbilectomy" at Cedars-Sinai Hospital in Los Angeles. An anonymous source helped spread the Gere gerbil myth with fake press releases supposedly issued by the Association for the Prevention of Cruelty to Animals, claiming that the actor had abused the small creature.

***Response.*** All indications point to the conclusion that gerbiling is simply an unverified and persistent urban legend

243

- that is, it is pure fiction.

Mike Walker, a journalist working with the National Enquirer, devoted months of effort in seeking to verify the gerbiling rumors about a celebrity. "I've never worked harder on a story in my life," Walker told the Palm Beach Post in 1995. After much hard work, he was unable to find any evidence that a gerbilling incident ever happened: "I'm convinced that it's nothing more than an urban legend."

Urban legends proliferate about celebrities, especially gay ones. A fairly innocuous example is the rumor that Rock Hudson, the movie star, and Jim Nabors, a television personality, were married in a ceremony in San Francisco. This story emerged in the 1970s, and has persisted ever since. There is no truth in it - except for the fact that both Hudson and Nabors were gay, though both were closeted at the time. Now at last in 2013 Nabors has gotten gaymarried, but to another man, his Hawaii companion of thirty-eight years standing.

Some stories of this kind are hoaxes, meant as exercises in humor. An example is the November 2012 claim that a 47-year-old gay man was arrested at San Francisco International Airport after ejaculating while being patted down by a male TSA agent. "Percy Cummings, an interior designer from San Francisco," was held without bail after the alleged incident, "charged with sexually assaulting a Federal agent."

"According to Cummings' partner, Sergio Armani, Cummings has 'multiple piercings on his manhood' which were detected during a full body scan. As a result, Cummings

244

was pulled aside for a pat-down. Armani stated that the unidentified TSA agent spent 'an inordinate amount of time groping' Cummings, who had apparently become sexually aroused. Cummings, who has a history of sexual dysfunction, ejaculated while the TSA agent's hand was feeling the piercings. The TSA agent, according to several witnesses, promptly called for back up. Cummings was thrown to the ground and handcuffed."

The use of names, such as Cummings and Armani, lends a spurious air of authenticity to such accounts. Still, this "report" was merely a spoof.

**BIBLIOGRAPHY**. Jan Harold Brunvand, Encyclopedia of Urban Legends, enlarged edition, Santa Barbara: ABC-CLIO, 2012.

# Conclusion

By contrast, most of the memes discussed in the above texts present serious challenges. Some are even plausible - at least they have long passed as such. Seemingly part of the conventional wisdom, they blend some bits of genuine observation with a sharp edge of aspersion. Advancing under the cover of a seemingly logical chain of evidence. they end up by asserting various claims that are in fact highly doubtful, as has been seen. Sadly, in many cases the flaws, even glaring ones, have not endangered their longevity. Some anti-homosexual memes have been advocated with such convincing aplomb that they pass muster even today–at least in some quarters. They have been around so long that "they must be so." In addition, they offer True Believers the satisfaction of enrolling themselves in the ranks of morality and decency–over against those who would subvert the basic principles of our society. These attractions, dubious as they are, show why it has been necessary to examine them at some length.

The sheer abundance of the homonegative motifs disgussed above is disconcerting: there are some two score of them. Readers may think of others that might have been included. By itself alone, this multiplicity is remarkable. There is no single mass of prejudice called Homophobia with a capital H that is vulnerable to straightforward attack and refutation. As we have seen, each motif needs to be studied for its own sake as an autonomous unit. Yet recognizing this inherent self-sufficiency does not preclude noting overlaps and composites. There is also a characteristic dialectic

246

in the passage of some ideas from the religious sphere to the secular and back again. Some gay activists, especially those who incline to atheism or agnosticism, assert that all the homonegativity in Western civilization stems from religion, especially Christianity.

As noted in the first meme discussed in Part One - the "unnatural" allegation - many are secular in origin. To be sure, following the principles of evolution we have often noted in our monitoring, this Platonic idea migrated into Hellenistic Judaism and then into the thinking of the apostle Paul. Since the hydra of homonegativity is composite and not some unitary entity, attempts to trace it to a single root, whether psychological or cultural, are misguided. Similar skepticism, alas, is also warranted with regard to the hope of finding a "magic bullet" that would destroy the hydra. Instead, each tentacle must be disabled separately.

Some academics working in the field of social psychology have ascribed the origins of homonegativism to two main factors: an authoritarian upbringing (especially a religious one); and a nagging fear that one might oneself be a latent or repressed homosexual. Both assertions are difficult to demonstrate. Moreover, even if the role these factors could be confirmed, the results would tell us little about the specific rationale for the adoption of this or that of the forty or so homonegative motifs. There is no substitute for examining and refuting them, one by one.

# About Wayne R. Dynes

Wayne R. Dynes (born August 23, 1934) is an American art historian, encyclopedist, bibliographer, and gay activist. He is now Professor Emeritus in the Art Department at Hunter College in New York City, where he taught from 1972 to 2008.

Dynes spent his early years in Southern California, attending public schools. After extended sojourns in Italy and England, he settled permanently in New York City. He obtained his B.A. at the University of California at Los Angeles in 1956; his Ph.D. at the Institute of Fine Arts of New York University in 1969.

During the 1960s Dynes was a member of the Mattachine Society of New York (MSNY). After the Stonewall Uprising (1969), he collaborated with his close friend Jack Stafford, a librarian, on a basic bibliography of gay studies. Ultimately, his dedication to this task yielded his tome *Homosexuality: A Research Guide* (New York: Garland, 1987). This accomplishment led to Dynes' service as editor-in-chief of the *Encyclopedia of Homosexuality* (New York: Garland, 1990). A major achievement, this two-volume set ranks as the first work of its kind. The *Encyclopedia* garnered six major awards, including three from library organizations.

For a number of years Wayne R. Dynes was active in the Gay Academic Union, editing and publishing its periodical *The Cabirion* (also known as *Gay Books Bulletin*). Since

2004 Dynes has conducted his own Internet blog at:

*www.dyneslines.blogspot.com*

www.ingramcontent.com/pod-product-compliance
Lightning Source LLC
Chambersburg PA
CBHW030302290526
45785CB00001B/189